A WOLF CALLED MOTKA

BY

STANLEY A. MOORE

Fayetteville Floral Publishing Co.
Fayetteville, WV, USA

A WOLF CALLED MOTKA
by
Stanley A. Moore

Library of Congress Catalog Card #96-61463

ISBN 0-9655251-0-4

Published by:

Fayetteville Floral Publishing Co.
101 W. Maple Ave.
Fayetteville, WV 25840-1401

Printed in the United States of America

ACKNOWLEDGMENTS

Although this book is a work of fiction, valuable technical assistance was generously donated by Pat Tucker, a wildlife biologist and Director of Wild Sentry, The Northern Rockies Ambassador Wolf Program, Box 172, Hamilton, Montana 59840. Pat and her gray wolf, Koani (pictured on cover), present a wolf educational program which reaches more than 20,000 people annually. It should be pointed out that the fictional content of this story is certainly not of Pat's doing. Her work is definitely nonfiction.

Also, I am indebted to John Rich, Butte, Montana for keeping Montana newspaper clippings flowing pertaining to the Wolf Recovery Program in Yellowstone National Park and central Idaho.

Additionally, a number of people gave graciously of their time in an effort to make this book literate and acceptable. For this, special thanks should go to Bobbi Taylor, Denise Light, and Donagrace Addington.

Alpha male gray wolf footprint - actual size

FOREWORD

Despite the fact that relatively few Americans have ever seen a wolf in the wild, probably no North American wild animal is better known. Because of their inherent ability to hunt in packs they are the most voracious animal predators in the history of this country. This dubious distinction may account for the fascination and interest that has followed wolves for centuries.

Over the years wolves have been both romanticized and vilified. Human imagination has made them the subject of fairy tales to classic novels. Conversely, their carnivorous and predatory habits made them the scourge of the cattle and sheep industries in the early years of this century which resulted in concerted efforts to eradicate them.

Today, naturally occurring wolves in this country are considered endangered. Other than an established population in northern Minnesota, and a scattering of individuals and packs in the northern tip of Wisconsin and Michigan's Upper Peninsula, gray wolves (Canis lupus) are known to occur naturally only in Montana's Glacier National Park along with a few packs between the Bitterroot Range and the Rocky Mountain Front.

Efforts have been under way for several years to reintroduce gray wolves in the Yellowstone National Park and in central Idaho where it is believed they can be sustained by high counts of large game animals. This action is designed to reestablish natural ecosystems in the wilder regions of the country, and to let people observe and appreciate a wildlife species that is part of America's heritage.

In 1994, after approval of an environmental impact study and the designation of Yellowstone National Park and central Idaho as experimental population areas, the Northern Rocky Mountain Wolf Recovery Plan of 1987 was broadened and the U.S. Fish and Wildlife Service began making wolf releases in those designated areas. Much resistance to this project has been met from a variety of interests, and the success of the program will ultimately depend on the cooperation and acceptance of the plan by the citizens of the affected states.

Incredibly, during one year in our modern world, 20,000 species of plants and animals become extinct. For the well-being of our own species this cannot be allowed to continue. Particularly, the prospect of world annihilation of such magnificent creatures as the African elephant, the Asian tigers, the black rhinoceros, a myriad of major marine mammals, and the last vestige of our own wild America—the gray wolf.

The author

INTRODUCTION

Many decades before the white man inhabited North America, a tribe of Indians named Blackfeet roamed the northwestern prairie of this continent on lands now known as Saskatchewan, Alberta, and Montana.

So named by the Europeans because of their conspicuously blackened moccasins, their main sustenance, which included food, clothing, and shelter, came from the American bison. The white settlers also named these life-giving animals that thrived during those early times in large, thundering, nomadic herds feeding on the grasslands of the West, buffalo.

After the Spanish colonists brought the sinewy, fleet mustangs to the West, the Plains Indians turned them into buffalo ponies which greatly improved their ability to hunt down the massive animals.

Until the time of the buffalo pony, the Blackfeet were most successful in stalking the wary bison by using wolf skins covering their backs and heads. Buffalo would tolerate wolves coming close, but not the upright Indians.

Therefore, it became quite natural for an affinity to develop between the Blackfeet people and the gregarious wolves. The Blackfeet considered the wolves brothers and part of the equation of nature which assisted the Indians to live from the buffalo herds.

The great respect and regard for the wolves fostered by this age-old relationship gave rise to the story of a legendary wolf who was the leader of all the wolf packs.

He was said to be solid black and only traveled on the darkest of nights. For that reason few had ever seen him, although many had reported seeing his glowing yellow eyes in the night. However, many had heard the distant howls which bore the distinct and unmistakable harmonics of this fabled and mysterious animal. His calls were interpreted in many ways over the years by the Blackfeet, and became responsible to a great degree in shaping the early culture of these tribal Indians.

Some said he was as large as a bear and would force the fearful grizzly to leave the Blackfeet hunting grounds. Others declared he always left an abundance of the horned beasts for the Blackfeet people since they were the wolves' two-legged brethren. Still others insisted his distinctive calls would beckon them to where the hunting was good, or would warn them when it was best to lie comfortably in their lodges wrapped in the warmth of their buffalo robes.

Many stories of this highly acclaimed wolf persisted and grew for generations. The tribal elders would speak of him with high reverence during lodge council meetings, and chiefs would look for the yellow eyes reflecting beyond the campfires before deciding to hunt.

In times of famine, the Blackfeet would call upon this great wolf for guidance, and when the buffalo were abundant, they would leave many carcasses to be shared with their wolf brothers to show esteem for the wise leader.

The Blackfeet had given this mighty wolf a name. They called him Motka.

DISCLAIMER

This novel is a work of fiction. Any resemblance to actual persons, living or dead, events or places is purely coincidental.

Well, not entirely.

The Wolf Recovery Program in Montana, Idaho, and Wyoming is real, as is the setting for this book. Although fictional, this story contains much factual data relating to gray wolves.

Still, this novel must be viewed as fiction because the human characters are so blandly stereotyped and so remote to the way people of today conduct their lives. Individuals like those in this book don't live in our modern, sophisticated society.

Or do they?

Yet, unquestionably, the main character makes this story indisputable fantasy. Who could possibly believe such a wolf as Motka exists or ever existed? An entire tribe of Blackfeet Indians must have been terribly wrong.

Surely.

"What is man without the beasts? If all the beasts were gone, men would die from a great loneliness of spirit. For whatever happens to the beasts, soon happens to man."

Chief Seattle
(Suquamish tribe)

"Life cannot exist without the animals and the birds and the insects and the fish. It cannot exist without the trees and the grass. Nor without the water and the air. Only when all life is connected can all life exist. It is a great lesson human beings have not learned."

Billy Greateyes
(Blackfeet tribe)

CHAPTER 1

The brisk but steady late April wind was from the southeast. Coming across the rolling rangeland with just enough force to ripple the spring grasses, it climbed effortlessly up the steep slope of Bear Mountain and tumbled in rolling turbulence over the other side. It was a wind a lazy Buteo could soar on from the treeless plains to the rolling hills to the jagged peaks westward within a day's hunt. The casual flight could make the sudden geographical transition seem effortless and almost boring.

Bear Mountain was among the many beginning cusps marking the abrupt change from the wide, open range of central Montana to the Rocky Mountain Front to the west. Scattered, without order, they rose up like warning signs of what lay ahead.

Wolf had circled so the wind would be on his nose as he trotted quickly up a shallow coulee toward a shortgrass plateau on the north side of the imposing mountain. It was an area in which he had found hares before.

The southeast breeze had signaled Wolf the day before, telling him it was time to hunt. The wind direction would shift soon and an angry, belated final blast of winter would roar through from the northwest. All the wild creatures, large and small, would seek comfort from the harsh weather. The smallest would crouch in burrows and nests to be warmed by their own body heat. The more confining the space the more warmth they would enjoy. The great antlered beasts would bed down in thick cover or stand hidden in the confines of available windbreaks, their furnace-like body temperatures protecting them from the icy chill.

The movement of prey would cease, making it difficult for Wolf to find food for his family. Food had been scarce, and it had been a long time since he had been able to offer anything of substance to the mother of his five pups.

Constantly alert, ears forward and eyes scanning the landscape, he was using the wind to his advantage—listening and looking for the slightest sound or movement that would reveal a likely quarry.

The hunt was slow and methodical. Wolf had learned from experience that haste was nonproductive and sometimes very dangerous. Even though he was anxious to find food, an overriding wariness was constantly with him.

Suddenly he stopped in mid-stride, one foot poised to take another step. Some faint sound had reached his ears. Distant and alarming, it had sounded like dogs baying making the hackles on his back rise in an involuntary crawl of his skin. No other creature in the vicinity would have paid attention to it, but Wolf's ears were acutely tuned to these kinds of disturbing airborne messages. There was a rustling of branches on the sparse, low scrub nearby, and a high pitched whine echoed through the scattering of lodgepole pines encircling the high mountain. The great number of noises was making it difficult, but Wolf waited patiently until he could separate the wind sounds.

Cocking his head to one side, ears pricked and rock still, he heard it again, barely perceptible. There were three of them. One voice was deep and melodious, the other two sharp and high pitched. The baying was from the direction in which he had traveled but far beyond the den on the mountain from where he had started.

A stab of fear and shock ran through his body as he realized the barking hounds were not tracking his trail but more likely the track of the white female. He had left her with the five hungry babies the night before in search of food. The whimpering pups and the look of need in his mate's eyes had prompted the hunt as well as the approaching weather. The gray wolf had hunted north of the den all night without success and first light had found him near the spot where past experience had produced an abundance of rabbits. With this knowledge he had pressed on.

Wolf knew he was getting too far from the den but the look in the white female's eyes had haunted him and he could not bear to return to her without a kill of some kind. Even a rabbit would have satisfied her anguish temporarily. Now the sun was approaching midday and the horror of his mistake struck him like a steel lash. His stomach was churning, and a crushing dread was crowding his brain.

Wolf was running now taking giant, leaping strides. His mind was also racing. When he had not returned at dawn, the white female could have slipped down off the great mountain to the spot where they had seen the mountain lion kill a few days before. It had been a calf belonging to one of the multitudes of large, lumbering beasts herded together by the two-legs. Wolf had learned early in his long life to avoid kills made by other animals. It was how his father had died.

13

Also, he had learned never to prey on animals belonging to the two-legs. It always brought forth the hateful dogs and advertised his presence in an area.

It was the two wolves' fourth season of the prairie flowers in this southern territory and they had avoided detection all that time by faithful adherence to these self-imposed rules. Hunger had tested his willpower on many occasions, but his self-discipline had always prevailed.

Wolf was no ordinary wolf, neither mentally nor physically. Weighing over 150 pounds with canine teeth nearly two inches long, few of his brethren challenged his authority, and few of them failed to take his lead in following his cautious but firm leadership. It was why the north pack he reigned over had grown and proliferated over the years, bounding out into ever increasing numbers throughout the region as new packs were formed.

But the white female may not have had his resolve and could have been hunger-driven to the cougar kill. When he hadn't returned at first light, his mate may have become alarmed, and her hunger may have clouded her judgment. She could have ventured down the mountain in the direction where she knew food to be. The babies were quite young but in desperation she may have decided to leave them briefly. The dogs probably had been brought out to hunt for the rogue cougar and had stumbled onto his mate's trail leading back to the den.

The dreadful thought made Wolf's feet fly even faster. Dogs rarely presented a problem for wolves, especially Wolf. In his younger days he would deliberately entice a chase when the opportunity allowed. Once he had led a pack of hounds almost fifty miles before doubling back and losing them. Some of the dogs had never found their way back home.

Wolf had engaged in these spiteful games primarily because of the low regard and disdain he felt for dogs. Certainly they were not to be feared. They were mindless, capable of only two things — sniffing an animal's track and barking themselves crazy. It made it all the more frustrating knowing most of the animals they hunted were just as ignorant. Too stupid to use the very asset they possessed that could assure their survival — their feet.

The lazy cougar, when it heard the dogs on its trail would simply climb a tree and wait until the two - legs arrived to shoot it down. The brainless bear would not run but would turn and fight until the lightning and thunder was close enough to kill.

If the two-legs didn't protect them, all the dogs would die. They didn't have sense enough to feed themselves, depending on the two-legs to do even that.

But as easy as it was for Wolf to outdistance canine pursuers, dogs after a female wolf with pups were another matter. This was what was creating the fear in Wolf's heart as he bolted toward their mountain refuge. The white female would never abandon her offspring and flee. She would stand her ground and fight to the death.

It was the fourth litter she had given birth to on the high rock outcropping on Bear Mountain, and until now they had always felt reasonably safe and secure. The closest presence of the two-legs was far away on the grassy prairie floor to the south and had never been a problem during their summer visits. The isolation of the area had been the compelling reason to choose the high mountain to have their young, and over the years they had grown to feel free from danger on this solitary, remote retreat.

Struggling to the ridge top beyond which lay the shallow lair, Wolf paused, winded by the enormous effort to reach his family. Simultaneously, a shot rang out and the now distinct howling of the dogs had turned into frantic yelping. It was too late. Wolf felt a sour bile rise in his throat, and a wave of despair swept over him. Death was not new to Wolf, but it had never struck this close before.

Testing the wind, he circled slightly and moved cautiously forward, the sickening smell of dogs and two-legs assaulting his nostrils. The urgency had been quickly replaced with a prudent wariness as the heavy, wind-blown odor scalded his senses. Moving slowly to a slight rise about fifty yards from the den, Wolf could see clearly.

There were three two-legs and three dogs. One of the two-legs held a sack containing the squirming wolf pups. Another was holding the excited dogs on a chain. Pulling and tugging, they seemed likely to break away at any moment, and the hunter was having a hard time holding them. The other two-legs stood by holding the dreaded lightning and thunder. Wolf has seen the awesome mysteries of the lightning and thunder work and knew the long distance of its power. Somehow the two-legs had learned the secrets of the clouds which could send great bolts of lightning and thunder to the ground destroying massive trees and reducing them to small slivers. It was what made the two-legs so dangerous.

Finally, Wolf let his eyes rest on the white female lying unmoving on the wide, flat rock in front of their den. She appeared to be sleeping except for the crimson pool of blood widening under her head. Behind her near the den opening were the mangled bodies of two of the five pups.

The urge to attack the perpetrators of the senseless carnage was so powerful that Wolf had to close his eyes and call on every ounce of self-restraint in his body. Only by rooting his muzzle in the dry, rocky ground until it hurt could he muffle the cry of anguish and pain that threatened to burst from his lungs. Charging thoughtlessly forward would have ended his own life and accomplished nothing. There was no fear in Wolf's caution – only an overriding, inbred wisdom.

The two-legs were preparing to leave, and amid their strange muttering and the straining, yelping dogs, Wolf had not been heard. The stiff breeze had prevented his scent from reaching them.

Almost before they were out of sight down the steep incline, Wolf was at his mate's side. A helplessness washed over him mixed with frustration and devastation as he sniffed her body. She was lifeless but still warm, and with a soft whimper Wolf covered her form with his own. It was all he could offer her.

Some instinctive, primal need for her warmth and strength consumed him. Her soft, warm presence under him and a rush of memories of their long term of life together let him endure the pain. The memories flooded his mind as he lay thus, feeling her small body slowly growing as cold as the waning gray day. A grief unlike any he had ever experienced gripped his heart. Even the death of his father paled beside the trauma he was now feeling.

Wolf had become the alpha male of the north pack with the death of his father. He vaguely remembered his mother and would never know the story of her tragic death, but he had run at the side of his father almost as far back as he could recall.

During the aging patriarch's final two seasons of the white rain, Wolf had protected him from the other younger males that occasionally felt a need to test the older wolf's leadership. Wolf had bided his time, content to govern the clan from the sidelines by keeping a quiet order among the more fractious members. None of the wolves dared to challenge Wolf. He was, through some hormonal or genetic quirk of nature, about half again larger than the other males. The old leader, huge himself, had sired most of the pack males, but none was foolish enough to confront Wolf. Wolf's size was sufficient to cower the most aggressive in the band, and if that wasn't enough, his quick, fearless snarl of dominance displaying the two inch fangs most always sufficed. Rarely was it necessary to go beyond that point because members of the north pack were extremely intelligent animals. They had witnessed his terrible ferociousness on many occasions, and they all possessed the mental capacity to understand the persuasion of facial expressions, growling, posturing and the displaying of fangs. It precluded the necessity for more violent behavior where a pack member could get hurt.

Jet black in color, Wolf's eyes were a glaring, icy yellow that could penetrate a grizzly bear's brain and send a spasm of abject fear to its heart. When Wolf made eye contact with hapless prey, they most always recognized and welcomed death. As Wolf aged, his muzzle turned white giving him the appearance of frothing at the mouth which in itself was adequate to settle most disputes.

As the old pack leader's tenure wound down, Wolf had guarded him closely and had offered guidance whenever possible. The older wolf's senses of smell, sight and hearing had steadily diminished with time, and the end had come when he had walked into a steel trap that had been baited with the discarded organs of an elk.

The struggle for freedom had been brief, and acceptance of his fate had displayed the old wolf's inner strength. Wolf had stayed close throughout the cold day and even colder night. During the afternoon of the second day, they had heard the trapper approaching, his traps clanging together over his shoulder.

Courageously, the aged warrior rose to his feet despite almost total fatigue brought on by the cold and the numbing pain from the hard steel's grip. The two had exchanged farewell looks, and the old leader had turned to face the hateful adversary.

The proud look of dignity displaying no fear would forever burn in Wolf's memory. It was his father's final message to him. Subtle but unmistakable, it had taught Wolf that real leadership didn't cease when life ended but, by example, continued its unique influence long after death came. The old wolf in his last minutes of life had demonstrated the courage and spirit that Wolf would need to be successful as the leader of the north country pack.

Waiting until the last minute, Wolf had disappeared at a trot, and before he had gone a hundred yards, he had heard the lightning and thunder. Wolves were always spared the indignity of death from old age. It was the only consolation Wolf could summon as the terrible pain of loss coursed through his body. Then he was running. Running until the cold was no longer there and the ache in his heart was bearable.

****

In Wolf's fourth season of the white rain in the north country and as alpha male of the growing pack, a young female rose in dominance in the clan. Her stunning beauty

19

was accentuated by her unusual coloring. Almost white but with enough gray to give her coat the look of silver, she was as distinct among the others as was Wolf with his contrasting blackness. She was small but fiery, and as she grew few males made the mistake of over-familiarity. Those that did inevitably ended up regretting it. It was as though she knew who her mate would be at the proper time, and it quickly became clear to the entire pack that it would be Wolf.

That was the year they found their own territory four hundred miles south of the pack's normal range. It was very uncommon for the alpha male and his mate to go off on their own for whelping, not to mention the unheard-of distance. But then it should be noted that Wolf and the white female were very uncommon wolves.

The need for numbers was instinctive and was particularly necessary during the season of the white rain. Only by hunting as a group during this time was it possible to survive. Although packs rarely exceeded fifteen wolves, the greater the total the more successful they could be in bringing down large animals. And, of course, large animal kills were essential in order to feed large counts of wolves. Being social animals, they were instinctively drawn together, and their gregarious nature bound them together like an invisible umbilical cord.

It was the epitome of wildlife family values, and it was why Wolf and the white female always returned to the north country when the threat of the white rain came. No matter how attached they became to their own newly discovered territory to the south, the first hint of cold weather would trigger the desire for their own kind, and they would begin the long trek northward, their noses living compasses.

Wolf's obligation as the alpha male made it imperative that he lead the pack. It was a time for reunion and for the introduction of new blood into the north family. Until this year Wolf and his mate had always added half a dozen youngsters to the group. Their careful nurturing had overcome the normally high mortality rate among wolf pups, and it offset the ongoing decline in the pack population from the hazards of an exceedingly hostile environment.

Many that separated from the pack never returned. Some were injured and subsequently starved or died from infection. The rigors of the hunt were arduous. The sharp antlers and hooves of their larger prey could inflict life-ending wounds. A broken shoulder or leg meant slow death, but the gnawing hunger forced exposure to these dangers. Few shirked their duty. There were no cowards in Wolf's north country pack.

Most that perished, however, died from the lightning and thunder possessed by the two-legs. Nevertheless, for many years the pack maintained healthy numbers due in large measure to Wolf's strong leadership and sound judgment. In fact, his wise parental guidance had been so successful over the years that the pack had splintered with uncommon regularity. With a normal contingency of eight to twelve members, pairs would break away and form their own families which evolved into new and growing packs.

The north country was vast, and new spoor boundaries were constantly being established in the boundless wilderness to the north. The quest was for dominance which meant far away from the two-legs.

****

Clouds had begun to thicken signaling the approaching cold front, and the late afternoon had turned gray and bitter. Darkness would come early this night. Already Wolf's eyes were beginning to grow heavy, and only the white female lying beneath him was being remembered. The white female racing at his side. The loyalty and devotion she had given him during her short life. Their time together on the high mountain had given them peace and comfort for longer than they had ever expected. Even the terrible cold and incessant hunger during the white rain season in the north were being recalled with warm nostalgia because the white female had been there beside him.

As Wolf pressed close to his mate's lifeless form, his tired eyes viewed the distant landscape now fading quickly in the darkening twilight.

A being much of his own image had lain here at a time before memory. A creation that had provided the miraculous opportunity for his own life. A million years ago? A thousand? Perhaps so short a time ago as a hundred years?

The now barren plain as far as the eye could see had teemed with life then. The thundering herds of bison made the rock on which he lay shake as they rumbled mightily forward like a dark, dusty, earth-bound cloud.

The antelope snaking in long, single lines through the valleys. The immense clusters of elk and deer. The solitary bighorn sheep and majestic mountain goats roaming the high peaks to the west making themselves visible on every mountain top.

The world was alive with life then including his own kind. But the two-legs had come, and the throngs of wildlife had all but disappeared. Until few but Wolf and the white female remained in this land of the two-legs. And now there was only Wolf amid a pitiful scattering of fearful remnants of an earlier time.

And instead of great numbers of wild and free horned beasts, there were now the pathetically docile and placid two-legs' animals. Content to move lazily to the next blade of grass and willing to be restricted without rancor by the long wire with which the two-legs seemed obsessed. The two-legs' singular purpose as they hurried about their nest of shelters being in containing the slow, plodding animals which if they had a mind to could easily trample the flimsy barriers without losing a stride.

Wolf had seen great numbers of these lumbering creatures milling together outside the confines of the long wire and free of all constraint. Yet, they had not attempted to escape. Why the two-legs spent their time trying to contain the great herds was an eternal mystery.

The two-legs possessed many powers but little wisdom, concluded Wolf as his reflections grew foggy and dream-like. He had not slept in the last two days, and the mad dash back to the den had finally taken its toll. His last thought before gracious sleep blanketed his pain was that he and the white female would not be adding new members to the wolf pack this season. And the white female would not be returning with him to the north country.

CHAPTER II

Two Jeeps came racing out of the north pasture from the direction of Bear Mountain. They were filled with hunters and dogs. Buck Dawson, foreman of Rogers Ranch, sauntered across the barn lot toward the parking area where the Jeeps would be pulling in. He had elected not to participate in the cougar hunt knowing it would be futile. The young calf had been dead for two days before it was discovered, and the cougar tracks would be dead cold.

Yet, the speed of the approaching vehicles suggested something had happened. Rooster tails of dust following the bouncing Jeeps indicated great haste. Dawson was an old hand at hunting for the big cats so he was skeptical. Age, along with growing up in the Montana Big Sky country, gave him a wealth of experience the other younger hands lacked. Although he was sixty-five years old, he could still ride and rope with the best of them and the spurs he wore every day were for much more than jingling when he walked. A big, robust man, the respect he enjoyed from his younger charges could be attributed more to this soft, no-nonsense demeanor than his size. Without any perceived effort he kept the entire ranch crew in line and the daily chores running smoothly and efficiently.

Buck Dawson had been Colonel Roland Rogers ranch foreman for over thirty-five years, having come to the Rogers ranch as a seasoned bull rider on the rodeo circuit. "Hard as nails and tough as pig iron" was an apt description of the burly cowboy. He was fond of saying he had been born in the dust, grew up in the dust, made his living in the dust, and would die in the dust. Literally dust to dust, so to speak, and he made every effort to live the part. Rarely would he be found, even on Sundays, not completely covered with range dust during daylight hours. A stomp of his boots before entering the mess hall or bunkhouse was all the cleaning they ever got. Even when it rained and the dust turned to mud, it had to wear off in the stirrups of his old ragged saddle.

Dawson's callous hands and deeply lined, sun-wrinkled face marked his trade, and a heavy mane of salt and pepper hair over steel-gray, gripping eyes gave him a rugged, almost romantic profile.

Buck was the oldest ranch hand on Rogers Ranch in terms of length of service, and only two other men had stayed on working for Colonel Rogers almost since inception of the cattle ranch.

One of these "old timers" was Pecky Woodall. Pecky had been Buck's sidekick on the rodeo circuit before Roland Rogers had hired Buck. It was during the initial period of hiring on the newly formed cattle complex, and Dawson had no trouble convincing the colonel that Pecky would be a good hand. Although a few years older than Buck, Pecky nonetheless could ride and cut cows as well as the younger men in those early days.

Thin as a racer and full of energy, there wasn't a lazy

bone in the man's body. Pecky's most distinct characteristics were his coal black hair, still in abundance now at seventy-two and a conspicuous, bobbing Adam's apple that did a dance every time he spoke. Which was often. He liked to talk. Although not well educated, Pecky possessed a sharp wit which he called on at every available opportunity. He was rarely caustic, and most of the men enjoyed his good natured and pleasant banter. When it was overdone or became tiresome, Pecky didn't become offended when a cowboy might ask him to shut the hell up.

Rounding out his more noticeable distinctions were the black, horn rim glasses which became necessary in his later years. They magnified his eyes giving him an expressively owlish look. It was a look more fatuous than wise, however.

A third man made up the ranch workers oldest trio. He was the Blackfeet Indian, Billy Greateyes.

Billy had ridden in one day about a year after the ranch commenced operations. His only possessions were wrapped in an old Indian blanket across the rump of his bareback pinto pony. Buck had hired the Indian but almost immediately regretted it. The lithe, bronzed Blackfeet could ride like the wind but couldn't rope or herd cattle worth a damn. Dawson didn't know this at first.

All the range people employed by Colonel Rogers were given a riding test by Dawson before being hired. It was Buck Dawson's criteria in determining potentially good cowboys. The test was always conducted on a bucker. Although there was a stigma attached to pulling leather – which was holding on to the saddle or saddle horn in order to stay on the horse – getting thrown was worse. A cowboy could pull leather and still be hired by Buck Dawson.

But after Billy Greateyes passed the riding test with flying colors, Dawson began including roping and cutting in consideration for employment.

Most all the ranch cowboys turned out to watch Billy's initiation and were summarily impressed. When the Indian slid off that bucking horse's back after his ride, a six year old could have ridden the animal in a Fourth of July parade— fireworks and all. The frazzled horse could have shaken molasses off his back easier than Billy.

But on the range Billy couldn't coordinate his intent with the horse's mind. Instead of rounding up cows, he would scatter them to hell and back.

Buck finally came to grips with Billy's problem without firing him. He assigned the Indian to the job of keeping the bunkhouse, kitchen, and mess hall clean. It was a chore none of the cowboys wanted to assume but a necessary one as Dawson was quick to discover once the ranch work force grew to fifteen men.

Buck expected the Blackfeet to quit but he didn't. To Billy, being janitor was no more demeaning than stringing fence or herding cows.

Actually, the Indian was happier in his new position. He was by nature a loner, and he could work by himself while the other men were on the range. He had established his own room by placing a cot in the woodshed near the kitchen. Only in the most severe weather would the Blackfeet creep into the warmth of the bunkhouse and then only to sit out the cold night on a rickety three - legged stool while wrapped in the faded, worn Indian blanket he had owned for years.

When Billy pulled the old blanket around him, only his wide pop eyes seemed to be visible. When open, his eyelids did not reach the irises, thus the whites of his eyes were always in a 360 degree circle of exposure. This wide-eyed expression gave the Indian a look of perpetual surprise and the appearance that he could not directly focus on anyone else's eyes. When he stared at one pair of eyes, it looked as if he were looking into the eyes of every person around him. What brought even more attention to Billy's eyes was the fact that they rarely blinked.

The eye characteristic was undoubtedly inherited. Perhaps his grandfather or great-grandfather had been named Greateyes. When census registration of the Indian tribes made it necessary to have a given name as well as a surname, Billy had seemed to be quite adequate and sufficient.

In the benefits package given to all Rogers Ranch employees, there had never been any mention of a pension plan. The jobs were so transitory they lacked enough permanency to consider a pension benefit. Few hands worked longer than a year or two. The remote isolation, the bitter cold winter work outdoors, and the long, hard hours were not attractive to modern day cowboys. The wages were above average for range work, but only the hardy applied.

Over the years only the three old timers had reached the length of employment whereby some type of pension loomed appropriate.

Buck Dawson had plenty of time in but was relatively young enough to continue performing his duties and be productive. He had no desire to retire, anyway. The truth was, he was indispensable since no one was being groomed to take over his job as foreman. It satisfied Dawson's modest ego.

Actually, age had made him a more effective manager.

The men respected him for his fair and impartial, albeit, firm assignments of duties. Plus, he could be tolerant of a little rambunctious behavior once in awhile so long as it didn't get too rowdy. Another factor contributing to his effectiveness as foreman was his willingness to work side by side with the hands regardless of the task and despite his advancing years.

Old Pecky Woodall was another matter. He had been one of Rogers Ranch's better cowboys over the years, but arthritis had taken him out of the saddle. Bent and twisted at seventy-two, he now could only putter around the ranch: straightening up, keeping equipment clean, running errands, and talking.

Of course, it should be said that he was a definite asset as a morale booster with his constant chatter. There was never any time for brooding in Pecky's presence, and if a hand got tired of listening to his talk, at least the man's woes would be sidetracked.

But Roland Rogers was a fair man. Gruff and feared by most of the younger men, the older ones were familiar with the cracks in his armor. He would continue to let Pecky live at the ranch and receive his three squares a day. The old cowboy had no relatives that he knew of, so what was Rogers to do? Take him in to Billings and drop him off on a street corner? Or place him in a homeless shelter?

Pecky would have screamed to high heaven if the colonel had forced him off the ranch. No one had any idea what the man had done with his money over the years. Even the amount of the Social Security check he received each month was unknown to anyone, and what happened to it was anybody's guess. Pecky liked to talk about anything and anybody – except himself.

Then there was old Billy Greateyes. He did nothing now except sit on his three-legged stool and stare into space.

In the early years, without warning Billy would ride off on his pinto pony for periods of up to two weeks. Where he went, no one knew. Or cared, for that matter. Then suddenly he would be back working as if he hadn't been away at all. It was exasperating for Buck Dawson, but he tolerated it. That is, until the old pinto died and Buck had made it clear that no ranch horse would be assigned to Billy. The Indian didn't argue about it. He was getting too old for such lengthy forays anyway.

Billy was the other old timer the colonel didn't know what to do with. Delivering him to the Blackfeet Reservation would be tantamount to taking him to the state penitentiary. Since Billy's needs were so meager, the colonel could not think of any reason to deny him room and board. After all, his room was a cot in the woodshed, and there was always plenty of food for an extra mouth. Billy didn't eat much and talked even less. And he certainly didn't get in the way. He kept to himself and seemed to prefer it that way. Getting a conversation started with the old Indian was next to impossible. Still, without the slightest warning, Billy would sometimes erupt into proverbial speech which always included ancestral authenticity and verification of his story. There were few on the ranch old enough or foolish enough to argue with what he said.

Pecky and Billy didn't know it but the colonel was a lot more benevolent than they suspected. He had long ago made preneed arrangements for them. A mortuary in Billings would handle Pecky's final requirements, and the Blackfeet Reservation Burial Committee in Browning would take care of Billy. Rogers could be accused of a lot of things but disloyalty to those who had served him long and well was not one of them.

The colonel wasn't worried about the ranch eventually becoming a welfare haven. The new breed of cowpokes like Cody Watkins, String Starcher, Ed Hastings, Whit Whittaker, and the myriad of other young workers that came and went, causing a bookkeeper's nightmare, would never be satisfied with permanency. They wanted to drift, move about, experience new places, and new situations. It was in their blood and was the nature of the young Montana cowboy.

A good number of them were rodeo hangers-on who didn't possess the talent to make a living at Montana's popular pastime. They would be attracted to the free room and board at Rogers Ranch which helped ease the hardship of range work, and they would stay until they got a few dollars ahead. Then the call of the rodeo would be repeated. They craved the cheering of the crowd and the excitement of the brief ride. It only made the extended solitude of range work harder to take.

Some would come back after a rodeo season or two looking for work again. Always a little more bruised and with a little less spirit. Most didn't know what they wanted out of life and had never given it much thought. Someday they would get old like Pecky and Billy, but it wouldn't be at the Rogers ranch, and it wouldn't be the colonel's problem. Rogers had often wondered what happened to old cowboys. He was taking care of a couple but what about all the others?

****

The Jeeps rolled in to the barn lot with a cloud of dust surrounding them. Six men and three dogs piled out, the men as loud as the excited dogs.

Colonel Roland Randolph Rogers turned to Dawson with a grin on his face.

"Found a bitch wolf and five young, Buck," he said with apparent pleasure. "Would you believe it?"

Dawson was silent, too dumbstruck to answer.

Cody Watkins, one of the hunters, eagerly started relating a long narrative of the hunt starting with how the dogs had hit the wolf trail at the remains of the dogie and rambling through the story to its eventual conclusion. Some of the other men pitched in with various salty details as Watkins stretched out the tale with obvious relish.

Only three men had followed the chase to the high mountain lair, the colonel and two other men content to remain in one of the Jeeps at the point where it could go no farther.

Dawson said nothing as he listened to the high pitched, excited voices. Instead, he walked over and peered into the gunny sack which was producing a cacophony of muffled whining and a lot of movement. It was a long moment before he assured himself that the young animals were indeed wolves. Recalling a wolf being in the territory took him back to his childhood years when he had the faint recollection of hearing a wolf howl. The memory had stayed with him only because his family had made such a fuss over it.

It should have been apparent to the happy hunters that Buck had not enjoyed the telling of the story, but they had been too engrossed in the yarn to notice.

"Why didn't you bring the bitch in? The wildlife people are gonna want to see her." Dawson was stunned by what he was hearing and seeing, but his reactions were purposely low key.

"She's up there if someone wants to drag her in. Hell, you can't sell no wolf hide now, Buck," Watkins answered.

"No, but you can dang well be put in jail for killing one." Dawson drawled.

As western cowboys go, Buck was not a particularly profane man. But he did have the odd habit of interjecting the word "dang" into most every sentence he uttered. This was certainly not offensive to the men he supervised who were accustomed to much saltier language. They hardly noticed the harmless practice.

The colonel stepped forward. "Nobody's going to be put in jail, Buck. In fact, her mate's probably up there somewhere, and we're going to get that son of a bitch too." By contrast, the colonel was a man of real profanity.

Watkins stood by with a satisfied look on his face. The colonel had spoken, and he knew he was on the right side of this fence.

Dawson wasn't going to argue with his boss, so he turned his attention to getting the dogs securely back in the dog lot. Somebody's hide was going to be nailed to the wall, he thought, but it dang sure wasn't gonna be his.

Colonel Rogers was tired as he slowly made his way to the back porch door of the massive stone house sitting apart from the other buildings on the ranch. He had been tall and thin as a young man, full of energy and vigor. But at seventy-five he had become stooped and dependent on a cane to get around. Gray and balding, his pale, slack face gave the appearance of gross inactivity. In his more ambitious days, he had expanded Rogers Ranch to become one of the largest and most prominent cattle ranches in the state of Montana. Although physically he had deteriorated, his mind had remained keen and analytical. But since the death of his wife a year earlier, he had become difficult and argumentative. So much so that his men made every effort to avoid him if at all possible, and only Buck Dawson and the colonel's daughter, Susan, seemed capable of dealing with him. The colonel had always been outspoken and opinionated, but age and his wife's death had exacerbated the problem.

Roland Rogers had separated from the Army Air Force at the end of World War II as a full colonel and immediately had fallen head-over-heels in love with a New York debutante by the name of Rose Alice Stinett. Of course, he had known she was a lady of substance and breeding but in the beginning had not known to what extent.

He was hopelessly in love before he learned that Rose's family was the legendary Stinett family of railroad fame in the last century. For that reason alone he couldn't be accused of marrying Rose for her money.

Not that anyone had suspected that being the case. Rose's parents liked the seemingly ambitious young officer, and Rose had quickly been caught up in his romantic overtures. The war had ended, and the entire nation was deliriously happy. The marriage had been a predictable part of the natural order of events in postwar America in the middle of the twentieth century. It was a period of the most per capita marriages, percentage wise, in the history of the country and would set the stage for the baby boomer phenomenon later in the century.

Rose Stinett was attractive. Saying she was beautiful would have been too charitable, but her blond hair and clear blue eyes certainly put her in the pretty category. She lacked the vivacious and lively nature of the social set she followed, but for Colonel Rogers she was his kind of woman. Down to earth and quite mature for her age, she was a thinker before she was a doer. Rogers recognized this characteristic which was what he wanted and needed in a mate to keep his own mistakes at a minimum.

The Stinett railroad had opened up the West, and the young-at-heart Rogers had the romantic idea of becoming a cattle baron on the wide open western prairie. He would raise them and the Stinett railroad would transport them to market. Why not capitalize on his good fortune in marrying into such a distinguished family? Being an asset to the family fortune would be expected of him and how better to do that than allying himself to the Stinetts in a related industry?

Even Rose thought it was a marvelous venture, so the idea had to be sound. Before she knew it, she had been talked into settling down after their marriage in one of the remotest parts of the fourth largest state in America – Montana.

Touted at the end of the twentieth century as the last best place, five decades earlier when Roland Rogers began putting his dream in place, it may have passed truthfully as the first worst place.

Even the early settlers of the West had hurried through the territory, although hostile Indians may have well played a deciding role in their haste. After the relatively easy passage over the level plains of buffalo grass and blue grama, the early warning signs of hard traveling ahead deterred very few in those early years. The flat prairie began to roll, trees began to appear, and the high mountains of the Rocky Mountain Front loomed ahead. Yet, the urge to move on westward afflicted almost all the pilgrims who saw this vast land and wide open spaces for the first time. It was the cursed cold, as Sam McGee would have said. So only a handful of the most hardy settlers terminated their odyssey in this land of frigid spaciousness. In time, the quixotic quest for elbow room and solitude by the American people, once the critical mass had been reached in more comfortable climes, made this great land the last best place. Much like the slogan "Best Kept Secret", it should have been somewhat self-defeating, but Montanans didn't think so. Their unique countryside would attract only their own kind — hardy, strong, and principled individuals. They would come. Not hurriedly, but they would come. And they would be of a like standard. Maybe that's what would make it the last best place.

Roland Rogers was one of those.

With Rose's bona fides, there was no problem obtaining substantial funding, and although twenty thousand acres of grazing land seemed excessive to start off with, the colonel had big plans. As his cattle business exploded, he wished he had bought more.

Since their money was being made the modern way of stocks, bonds, and inherited wealth instead of the old-fashioned way of blood, sweat and tears, the risk of not being successful was less onerous. The consequences of failure never entered Roland Rogers' mind.

The ranch they built was a showplace for rural Montana. Even the governor came to their open house along with many other state and industry dignitaries. The main house was constructed primarily of Montana stone — ranch style, of course. Ten thousand square of it. The massive stone steps, ten feet long, had been brought in individually on a tractor-trailer and unloaded by a crane with a twenty-foot boom. The crane was used to place the steps, the large fireplace stones in the great room and kitchen, and the huge polished rafters of the cathedral ceiling which beamed down over half the house.

Although conspicuously magnificent architecture, the structure managed to present a rustic facade which somewhat toned down the appearance of palatialness.

Five bedrooms with individual baths, a study with adjoining library, a great room, a dining room, and an immense kitchen were the basics. A west wing consisted of an office complex where the ranch business was conducted.

It appeared a deliberate effort had been made to avoid pretentiousness. All the material comforts and conveniences were on a luxurious scale but tastefully inconspicuous so a feeling of hospitable warmth was present. Not elaborate to satisfy the eye but designed to give real pleasure and enjoyable living.

The barn could accommodate forty horses although it was rarely filled with only horses. Most days there were also a few winter chilled or orphaned calves occupying stall spaces.

The elaborate apartment-style "bunkhouse" could house twenty cowboys but had never been full. The ranch work force normally peaked out at around fifteen men. A kitchen and mess hall afforded the amenities.

It was two years before the facility was ready for occupancy, the long miles of wire stretched, and the paddocks built to corral their genesis herds of white-faced Herefords and Red Angus beef cattle.

The colonel had prided himself in the independence of utilizing only his own land instead of the publicly-owned open range to graze his cattle. Cows drifted too far without fences, and during an unusally late spring, calving loses could be astronomical. Young calves could not be found when late winter storms developed if the herds were not carefully collected and accounted for. This was the busiest time of the year for the cowboys with twelve to fourteen hours in the saddle not uncommon. The herds were monitored daily, and debilitated newborns in the windswept snows were brought in across saddle horns to the warmth of the barn. Only by fencing and paddocking was this possible. Putting meaningful worth on a newborn calf helped balance the ledger sheet and maximized the prosperity of Rogers Ranch. It also gave the colonel a sense of comfortable independence which he quietly enjoyed.

Rogers had heard that open range land could be grazed down to the point where it took twenty acres to support one cow. He didn't want any part of that. He would raise his own cattle, and he would grow his own grass.

Starting out on a small scale, he began an irrigation system from a tributary of the Musselshell River, experimenting with growing alfalfa and some of the wild grasses. The stream was close by and strategically located for irrigation of his prime fields. The venture proved to be an enormous asset in livestock production and reduced labor costs.

The long rows of stacked hay dotting the landscape like giant, brown loaves of bread soon became a trend in hay production in Montana and Roland Rogers' stature as a livestock producer grew as fast and as long as his hay stacks.

Of course, during a dry summer he didn't mind letting his cattle move around more freely. He paid enough taxes to take advantage of a little cheap public grazing land occasionally. Everybody else did it so why shouldn't he? Wherever the best grazing could be found was best for the cattle and therefore best for everyone concerned.

But whenever the winter winds howled and the snows flew, the colonel was careful to round up his stock and deposit them in more manageable compounds. Feeding them substantially and improving production figures.

It was a grand plan for Roland Rogers but not, ultimately, for Rose Rogers. The colonel had selected his land with great care as far as cattle raising was concerned but had not given much thought to its isolation and the convenience to a decent size town. Billings, the closest city, was Montana's largest but was located eighty miles to the south. This meant eighty miles from what Rose considered the nearest civilization.

Over time, the remote living took a toll on her. This was one decision she had made without thinking it through. Colonel Rogers may never have known her regrets in agreeing to move to such isolation. She had always prided herself in cautious decision making and would never have admitted to her husband she had made such a monumental mistake. Not one to complain, she endured the unhappiness for years. When she became pregnant and gave stillbirth to a son, it only added to her melancholia.

Miraculously, five years later she presented the colonel with a beautiful and perfect baby girl. They named her Susan Margaret after both grandmothers. Susan brought to her mother a modicum of peace and tranquility that at last seemed satisfying, and this sustained Rose Rogers' contentment through her last years. For the colonel the child brought great happiness and pride, and he doted on her. Not only had Rose become trapped by the isolation, but her husband also had felt the despair that loneliness brings. Susan was the catalyst that rescued not only Rose but Roland as well.

A private tutor was brought in for the young girl's elementary education, and there was some discussion of sending her abroad for her advanced learning. If not that, at least Bryn Mawr or Wellesley. In the end Susan made the decision herself. She wanted to do something meaningful with her life, and when she announced her choice of the University in Missoula followed by medical school, both her parents were shocked. The young, headstrong girl had gotten her way, however, and secretly both the colonel and Rose were proud of her.

****

The colonel stomped through the back door to find Susan sitting at the kitchen table with a cup of coffee in her hand. She was dressed in faded jeans, dusty riding boots and a grungy-looking old sweat shirt about two sizes too large. But from the neck up she looked like an angel from heaven.

Blond and blue-eyed, she radiated loveliness. Although thirty, she could have passed for twenty. It was obvious she was an outdoors person, not only due to her attire but from the sun-kissed complexion of her face. It made for a startling beauty accentuated by warm, full lips and white, even teeth.

But it was the clearness of her deep, blue eyes that was the focal point of her grace and charm. Her delightful voice added to the aura of her beauty, and it gave her speech a vibrant quality which made her face sparkle. Seeing how she was dressed, no one not knowing her would have suspected she was a medical doctor.

She was nearly ready to go to the barn to groom her bay gelding.

"Hi, Dad," she greeted warmly.

The old man only grunted as he fell into a kitchen chair. The bouncing Jeep had worn him out during the long hunt.

Rozi, their cook and housekeeper, was sitting across from Susan polishing silverware. She gave a halfhearted acknowledgment to the colonel and continued with the polishing. Rozi, a full-figured and tall middle-aged woman, was the wife of Pancho Rivera, the ranch handyman. Her full name was Rozita Marie, but everyone called her Rozi.

With long, black hair pulled around and clasped tightly at the back, she looked more American Indian than of Mexican origin. The round face, ruddy complexion, and dark eyes only added to the perception.

Rozi and Pancho had come to Rogers Ranch the year Susan was born. Ostensibly, to help Mrs. Rogers with the added burden of a new child and to allow the colonel to free up more valuable manpower for cattle work. Having cowboys trim shrubbery and mow grass was not good economics, to say nothing of maintaining high morale.

It turned out well. The colonel could not have found a more dedicated pair. Both were perfectly matched for the jobs they were hired to do.

Buck Dawson immediately saw that Pancho was more than just a handyman, and before he had worked a month, he was in charge of the commissary and driving in to Billings once a week for supplies and the mail.

Rozi, it turned out, was an excellent cook and

housekeeper. More importantly, both of the Riveras were pleasant, happy, and hard working. Young Susan became an important part of their lives which helped the young child to overcome the handicap of growing up without peers. The colonel thought Rozi and Susan spent an inordinate amount of time together which prevented Rozi from getting much done around the house. They were the only women on the ranch but Rogers never considered their need for woman talk. The truth was that Rozi didn't care much for the colonel and usually had very little to say to him. Her propensities were for happy, fun loving people. The colonel never demonstrated such behavior, seemingly always quarrelsome and in a sour mood. But she loved "Missy" which was the name both Rozi and Pancho had been calling Susan since she was a little girl. Missy always had a smile on her face and rarely had an unkind word even when annoyance was evident in her features. Undoubtedly, it was an offshoot of being brought up under the influence of the affable and jolly Rozi and Pancho.

"Did you find the cat?" Susan asked cheerfully. She had not heard the flurry of activity outside with the return of the hunting party.

"Better than that, Sweetheart. We got a bitch wolf and five pups," he chortled.

Susan almost dropped her cup.

Rogers was keenly aware of his daughter's sensitivity, and his demeanor around her was always different than with other people. He immediately knew, in his self-satisfaction, he had not chosen his words carefully.

"What happened?" she whispered with alarm.

"The dogs got to a couple of the pups before we could

get there to stop them. We brought the others in." He couldn't stand to look at her so he dropped his eyes to the floor. "We had to destroy the bitch." The old man was trying to interject a conciliatory note after realizing how caustic his remarks must have sounded to his daughter.

Susan was out the door before he had time to look up again. She saw the knot of men gathered around the barn entrance and dashed in their direction. She didn't have to look far. Faces were peering down into an old galvanized washtub, and one man was poking the furry, wailing babies with a stick.

"You men can get back to work now. I'll take care of these pups," she announced, surprising the workers with her sudden appearance.

The startled men fell back like the plague had suddenly risen out of the washtub to smite them.

"You stay, Pancho," she added, seeing the old Mexican handyman hanging in the background trying to get a look at the young animals.

She wasn't mad. After all, probably none of the men had ever seen a real live wolf before and neither had she. But she was definitely upset with her father. What he had done was unconscionable, and it was making her almost physically ill.

"Get a clean saddle blanket out of the tack room, Pancho. And clean out that first stall. One of those dogs gets loose and these little fellows are history."

She looked the frightened wolves over carefully. It was obvious, judging from the manner of their distress, that hunger was the main reason for their immediate discomfort. She could remedy that, she thought confidently. Caring for young animals at Rogers Ranch as she was growing up had been her specialty and eventually her unofficial but expected job. Kittens, puppies, orphaned wild animals, and dogies. She had even raised her gelding, Little Joe, on a bottle when the intractable old mare had refused to let the foal nurse. They had hobbled the mean spirited mare and milked the colostrum from her. Then for three months, every four hours Susan had fed the playful little colt from a bottle.

And look at him now, she reflected. Fifteen hands, sleek and eager to go. His own mother could not have done a better job even had she been so inclined.

She remembered the time when she had first slid onto his back, expecting the intrepid three-year-old to promptly dump her in the barn lot with all the hands looking on. She had no idea of the drama that had been building for months among the cowboys contemplating the moment.

When time came to break the high-spirited colt, the subject of who would do the honors began to gather momentum among the bunkhouse crew. Each hand had secretly wanted to be Miss Susan's choice of riders.

Buck Dawson had felt he would be the one chosen in deference to his status as foreman. Being the most experienced hand as well as the one closest to Miss Susan made him the logical choice. At the same time, he dreaded the chore. He hadn't busted a bronc in years, and although he could still ride and rope well, he had lost some measure of confidence in his ability to get the job done without embarrassment. Deep down, Buck had tried to assuage the growing suspicion of a waning of intestinal fortitude without actually admitting it to himself.

At that time Cody Watkins, String Starcher, and Ed Hastings were cowboys who had only recently joined the Rogers ranch work force, and all three had immediately fallen in love with the comely young maiden home for spring break from college. All harbored a secret fantasy that Miss Susan would choose them to ride the fractious colt thus solidifying their status in the bunkhouse hierarchy. It would satisfy each cowboy's curiosity as to which one Susan Rogers favored.

Cody Watkins, the youngest of the new men and suffering under the spell of romantic delusions for the pretty Rogers filly, wanted desperately to be the one to impress her. All his love affairs had been from afar, and this one was no exception. He seemed drawn to women who could ride horses. Why this attraction existed was anybody's guess, but it made Susan Rogers his kind of woman.

The short, wiry cowpoke with the mass of unruly red curls under his oversized cowboy hat always looked smaller than he was. This was mostly because all of his clothes were too big. The sleeves of his blousy shirts always covered his knuckles, and his billowing leather chaps dragged the ground when he walked. The long ringlets gave his face a childish look, and his high pitched voice added to that perception. He didn't look like a grown man, yet he seemed to take the lead in every group activity among the ranch workers.

String Starcher, well on his way to becoming a letcherous adult male hadn't given a thought to any difficulty riding the prancing colt but could only see the budding coed home from school for the summer. Rogers Ranch was not the most propitious place for girl watching, but the crass Starcher was going to make the most of it while he could.

Sandy haired with pale gray eyes, String's body did resemble a thread. He had no hips to hold up his pants and was constantly tugging on the belt loops to keep them in place. Even a tight belt didn't help. It had been suggested that he get a pair of suspenders but he thought that would make him look like an old man. Loud but likeable, String instigated much of the horse play indulged in by the men when boredom dictated it.

Then there was the quiet and self-effacing Ed Hastings who only wanted Miss Susan to like him. He would have ridden the horse through a ring of fire if it would have brought a smile from her in his direction.

Ed was somewhere in his forties but looked older than Buck. In cowboy jargon, he had been rode hard and put up wet all his life. The romance of his chosen line of work which was the rodeo hadn't lasted long, but he had stuck with it simply because he had no other skills and nowhere else to go. It was eight seconds of the most exhilarating ride a human being could ever experience, but it always ended with eight hours of getting over it. As Ed got older he was sometimes eight days recuperating from the short and not so sweet adventures.

Buck had hired Ed primarily because he had felt sorry for the forlorn-looking cowboy but had never had cause to regret it. Hastings had proven to be a good hand.

In the end, after all the lead rope work and the longeing and the colt getting used to a mild snaffle bit in its mouth, the nimble Miss Susan had simply led the dancing horse along side a plank fence in the barn lot, climbed the fence, and mounted the nervous animal bareback.

The entire crew had stood aghast as they watched the young girl trot the high-strung horse around the lot a couple of turns and then canter up the farm road toward the pet cemetery half a mile away . Not a word was said until horse and rider were out of sight.

"I hope they come back," quipped old Pecky. "I ain't

hankering to dig no horse grave although it won't be no fer piece to drag him." He was thinking of what the colonel would do if his daughter got hurt because of that snorting, high-stepping charlatan.

The damn horse had dashed the secret dream of every bronco buster on the ranch. Except Buck Dawson whose relief would never be suspected or publicly known.

****

Susan's care-giving supplies had been stashed away years ago but she remembered where they were stored. As she strode through the kitchen after returning from the barn, her father entered the room.

"I called the Fish and Wildlife office in Billings. They are going to send someone out in the morning to get the wolves," he said in a rather subdued voice. He sensed his daughter was upset with him and he wanted to make amends.

"If they aren't fed they won't be alive in the morning." she hissed, while digging into the top shelf of a corner cabinet.

The old man remained silent as he watched Susan heat the milk and prepare the three small bottles. The variety of nipples she found was extensive, and she was able to find three that were suitable and not deteriorated with age.

Returning to the barn with the prepared formula in the towel-wrapped bottles, she wondered if the wild things would nurse given the circumstances under which they had been removed from their mother. There surely had been a lot of trauma with the dog attack.

Pancho stood by in fascination with much apprehension mixed in as Susan thrust her hand into the mass of fur, found the nap of a neck, and pulled the largest of the squirming, twisting animals to her lap. The warm milk and soft nipple did its magic, however, and she was thrilled when the young wolf stopped struggling and began to suckle in earnest.

Susan had noted Pancho's look of anguish as she wrestled the slippery pup. The short, round Mexican with the handle-bar mustache had always been timid. The ranch handyman, he nevertheless carried considerable responsibility for the daily operation of the facility. He seemed always to be where he was needed and would cheerfully undertake any task assigned to him–most times with a twinkle in his eye and a smile on his face. Only with Rozi would he sometimes become impatient and quarrelsome. Probably because the ranch pecking order placed Rozi as the only person below him.

But it was clear he had no desire to help in the handling of the wolf pups.

"What's wrong, Panch?"

"Colonel Rogers ain't gonna like it if you lose a finger. Them things got teeth like a rattlesnake," he croaked.

"Panch, you know I've been handling little meanies like these for years," she reminded him.

"I know, Missy, but you ain't never bothered with no wolves before."

"You really have a way with words," she exclaimed with a roll of her eyes. The man was hopeless.

Quickly evaluating their sex, she noted that the two larger oatmeal pups were males while the smaller female was almost silver. As she stroked the fine hair of the little female as she sucked eagerly on the bottle, Susan was struck by her beauty. She was the last to be fed and had also accepted the warm milk.

Recalling her father's words of the hunt, tears sprang to her eyes. Considering the intelligence of the human species, what made it so difficult for so many to recognize the misery they sometimes wrought?

As the young wolf suckled noisily, she had the distressing thought that her father would never change. He had been brought up to regard all animals as merely commodities to be exploited and used. Never mind they could bleed, feel pain, hunger and occasionally pleasure. In his view they were no more than apples hanging from a tree. Their singular purpose to be plucked, eaten or discarded. Next year the tree would bear again, and there would always be plenty.

But an animal family might be terminated, succinctly and with finality, thus making the survival of a species ever more stressful and difficult.

Looking at the small, furry babies, quiet now with their plump bellies full of milk, Susan felt a disquieting sense of injustice which slowly filled her with a frustrating rage. Why wasn't her father capable of understanding that animals were not like fruit on a tree?

Just thinking about it made Susan want to cry.

CHAPTER III

It was dark when Wolf awoke. It took a moment for the reality of the tragedy to penetrate his brain, and he was momentarily startled to discover he was lying on top of his mate. Her body was cold and stiff now, so he stood and shook himself, the events of the day coming back to him in a rush of horrible detail.

He was convinced her strength had transferred to his body because the great fatigue he had felt before he slept had eased. Having not rested in two days plus the killing dash back to the den had taken its toll on his body, and the sleep had been essential.

Instinct told him it was early night. That meant there was plenty of time.

Pulling and tugging, he dragged his mate to the edge of the flat rock which overlooked the distant panorama of grass. From that vantage point they had sat together for hours gazing across what had become their domain. Rippling, golden grassland stretched as far as the eye could see to the south and east, and to the west rose the majesty of snow peaked mountains even higher than their own. He would leave her in eternal vigilance at their favorite spot in their chosen land.

They had never been disturbed by the two-legs or their dogs on this isolated mountain until now. Suddenly their contentment had been shattered for all time, and nothing could bring it back.

Their initial foray south had been carefree and exhilarating. After suffering through an exceptionally severe season of the white rain, a Chinook wind had brought a warm wave of spring-like weather to the pack. The band of wolves had ventured far up the Saskatchewan River on an instinctive quest for milder temperatures southward.

The white female, following the Chinook wind with the pack, was afflicted with a spring fever she had never felt before. It was brought on by her first season as the alpha male's mate and the maternal warmth of Wolf's babies in her womb. She was now dominant and Wolf ran obediently at her side.

The daily warming of the Chinook as they moved farther and farther south spurred them on. Finally, they broke away from the pack and headed due south, the white female leading the way with a heady sense of purpose driving her. Her time was close, and with the directional instinct of a bee martin she pointed her nose toward Montana.

Food had been plentiful due to the coincidence of passage through three wildlife refuges, and the direct south routing had avoided a long and hazardous detour around Lake Fort Peck. The long, sprawling reservoir of water of the Missouri River backed up by Fort Peck Dam would have taken two days of hard traveling to skirt.

A more cautious direction would have pulled them to the security of the western mountains, but the white female was enjoying the wide open spaces of the open range. Wolf had been nervous about the lack of cover but had let the white female have her head. There had been something exciting about running carefree in the open countryside during the crystal clear nights. It was something Wolf had rarely done, but now he was indulging his mate and feeling her joy.

Fate must have intervened in their finding the flat rock overlook on Bear Mountain just before the white female's time arrived. Working furiously, the two wolves had dug out their rudimentary den before their first litter was born.

There had been two more families, and now their fourth had been destroyed. The white female was gone, and there would be no more.

****

It was difficult to turn his back on his long-time mate, but there was nothing more he could do for her. He busied himself with a final chore. Carrying the pitiful remains of the two pups that had been attacked by the dogs to the back of the den, he covered their bodies with dirt. Some dry leaves and dead branches masked the den entrance. It was the best he could do.

Now he was ready. Even so, it was agonizing to leave. Only by thinking of the task at hand could he pull himself away.

Though it was dark he had no trouble finding the two-legs' place to the south. He had seen it many times, instinctively giving it a wide berth. He had always been curious about it. Not fearful, but cautious.

Why did the two-legs accumulate so many of the

bison-like animals, and why did they string the long wire around them? The sluggish, lumbering beasts could not run very fast and didn't seem inclined to escape. Their only interest appeared to be in eating the prairie grasses. Yet, the two-legs were constantly stretching and repairing the long wire to keep them confined. No animal that Wolf knew of could be stopped by the flimsy wire. He had jumped over and crawled under it on many occasions.

And why did they want the nasty-smelling animals? He had tasted the meat of one once and thought it terrible. Greasy and fat, it was not at all like the deer, antelope, and elk. Even a tough old moose was better. As Wolf had previously concluded, the two-legs lacked common sense but were in possession of some magical and little understood powers that made caution essential.

He had come to the first of two fences he would cross before arriving at the two-legs' shelters. Sliding under the wire on his belly was easy. Checking the wind, he circled slightly to get the wind on his nose. The night breeze had picked up, and the lack of stars and moon indicated a heavy cloud cover had moved in making the night dark. He would be compelled to rely on his nose for guidance.

The move to the west resulted in his approaching the ranch directly up the lane that led into the sprawling complex. There was no danger on the road at this time of night, but Wolf moved slowly with a wary alertness.

Two stone columns standing on each side of the roadway and designating the ranch entrance alarmed him. Circling, he avoided walking between the tall, slender markers towering out of the grass without purpose.

As he drew near, he stopped and studied the buildings. There was a main lodge where the two-legs slept. It was made of stone and had numerous trees and shrubs around it. Some distance away was another large building that housed the range horses that the cowherders rode. Wolf was to find this out later. Beyond that building were several smaller structures that quartered the ranch hands, a kitchen and dining room in which to feed them, plus a variety of storage buildings. Wolf knew none of this and didn't care. His attention was focused on finding where the dogs were located. The cold front would move through during the night bringing frigid winter air back again with clear skies. But for now, the clouds were making the night as black as Wolf's coat. This was in his favor except it would also make it difficult to find the dogs that were now silent. Wanting to get closer, instinctively he was crawling on his belly being guided strictly by his nose.

In spite of the late hour, there were several lights burning throughout the maze of buildings. There was danger being this close to the two-legs, but Wolf had a mission. A mission in which an element of danger was necessarily present. A mission of vengeance which could not be ignored. The white female deserved no less.

The breeze was bringing many scents to Wolf's nostrils, some quite foreign. The distinct odor of the range horses touched his nose forcefully, and he was aware that the large building directly in front of him was the horse barn.

The smell of horses was not new to Wolf. Many times he had crossed the unmistakable path of the wild herds of the plains. It was another mystery of the power of the two-legs. Horses were so free-spirited, powerful and fleet of foot. How were they captured and subdued so easily? Reduced to carrying the two-legs on their backs. The question flitted across Wolf's mind now only because he had given it much thought in the past.

Then somewhere in the mix of odd scents he was receiving from all directions, he smelled them. Dogs. They were close, at the back of the horse barn. The sickening odor was unmistakable, and a cold chill made his hackles rise. It was not born of fear but of a profound committed purpose. Circling again slightly to the west he moved imperceptibly, hugging the ground and hardly breathing. Closer and closer until he could see the three forms lying on the ground. All three dogs were attached to long lines that gave them room to move freely but prevented them from reaching each other. There was a small shelter for each dog, but none was in use. Instead, all three dogs appeared to be asleep on the cool ground just outside their houses.

Wolf was patient and methodical. Years of being the hunter had sharpened his stalking skills so necessary for success. First, he made sure they were all asleep, watching them closely for any sign of wakefulness. The strenuous hunt of the day probably had tired the dogs. The incessant barking alone would have sapped their energy. He was also trying to identify the leader, the big red hound with the deep resonance. He finally satisfied himself that the nearest dog was the one by virtue of its size. He was big but Wolf's rage and resolve removed that as a factor. The attack would necessarily be on the closest dog, and it was the one he despised the most. He was lucky.

Still he waited.

Several minutes passed before Wolf moved slowly forward again. Time was not important but stealth was. The ground was hard and bare with nothing to create a sound as he moved. There were no sticks, leaves, or loose stones. His progress was so slow that it appeared there was no movement at all. He wanted to get closer. He had all night. Quietly, out of the black night a giant, ghostly shape rose up from the ground not twenty feet from the red dog. It seemed to float through the air and engulf the sleeping animal like a smothering, black blanket. The only sound was when the great hulk slammed into the motionless dog and forced the air from its lungs in a shrill, whispering rush of air.

Big Red was suddenly aware of a crushing weight over his entire body and a terrible pain in his throat. He struggled to rise but could not get his legs under him because of the inescapable burden. There was no breath and he couldn't utter a sound. Instinctively, he desperately wanted to howl, but his lungs were empty. Something had clamped on his windpipe and was slowly suffocating him. Somewhere in a faraway background he heard other dogs howling frantically, but he couldn't answer.

There was great pain in his throat, and the heavy weight was terrifying. His legs were useless, and he had no strength to rise. His feet could only flail the air finding no purchase to lift himself erect.

Being unable to make a sound or escape from the intense pressure that pinned him to the ground brought fear to the red hound the likes of which he had never before known. The black cloak covering him was soundless but Red knew what it was. The escalating fear paralyzed his brain.

A whirling, screaming circle of white and black was drawing him to its center, and the barking had become a deafening, continuous roar of confusing noise. Then the roaring noise got fainter and began to drift into silence. The horrible fear began to fade, and the loud, spinning vortex in his head began drifting silently away. His legs had stopped all movement except for a twitching reflex.

Wolf held his grip on the struggling dog with all the power in his jaws, clamping him to the ground with his entire body. The other dogs had come alive and were piercing the night air with frantic yelping. It was doubtful they had heard the silent attack, but Wolf's scent had reached them, and they were now straining on their chains and going crazy with frustration from the nearness of the great wolf.

A light appeared on the front porch of the main house, and another was moving toward the barn from the bunkhouse. Wolf watched the two lights converge at the entrance to the barn. They would move toward the barking dogs next, and he would wait until the lights were at the corner of the long building before relaxing pressure and bolting away. The dog under him had stopped all movement, but Wolf would maintain a death grip until the last possible moment.

The colonel had been the person with the light that emerged from the main house. He had been in his study indulging in a nightcap when the dogs began to bark. Buck Dawson had come running from the bunkhouse. Dawson never went to bed early.

"What the hell are those dogs barking at?" demanded an irate Rogers when he met Dawson at the barn.

"Danged if I know, Colonel," the ranch foreman responded. "We better see what's going on."

The two men headed for the dog lot at the back of the barn, both flashlights bobbing with the swing of their arms. Quickly focusing the lights on Max and Beethoven, the two barking hounds were now on the fringe of hysteria. Then Dawson directed his light on Big Red. The red dog was stretched out in the dirt as if asleep.

"Jesus," he exclaimed in a whisper.

Both men stood over the still form for several seconds before Buck knelt down and touched the hound's neck.

"He's dead, Colonel."

Rogers was beaming his light out into the darkness in every direction, but there was nothing. The dark night closed around the weak light in less than fifty feet.

By now several more men had arrived asking what had happened in loud whispers. The colonel took charge.

"You men get back to the bunkhouse. You'll destroy tracks tromping around here. We'll wait until daylight and see what the hell it was. Pancho, get these yowling dogs in the barn. Shut them up if you have to use the water hose on them."

"Si, Colonel Rogers." Pancho jumped forward as if someone had lit a fire under him. As usual, he was Johnny-on-the-spot.

"Leave Red where he is. We'll examine him in the morning." With that, the colonel wheeled and hobbled slowly back to the house.

The men had retreated but only out of earshot of the colonel. They huddled together in a muttering mass as if some evil spirit was lurking in the dark around them. They all felt some unknown presence so mysterious and deadly that it defied discussion above a whisper. Something had killed Big Red right in the dog lot not a stone's throw from the bunkhouse. It took Buck Dawson's firm control to prod them as a group back from whence they had come. They moved reluctantly, unhappy with not knowing exactly what had happened.

Susan had heard the commotion as she was getting ready for bed. First, the barking dogs and then the men. She had dressed hurriedly and then thrown on a robe so she could quickly get outside. Her father was coming in the front door as she entered the hallway.

"What is it, Dad," she whispered.

The colonel had gone directly to the liquor cabinet. "That lobo killed Big Red," he stated with conviction. He had already made up his mind about what had happened.

"Oh, no! Dad, are you sure?" Her voice had a ring of incredulity to it.

"Damn right I'm sure. But don't worry; we're going to get that son of a bitch." He took two fingers of Scotch whiskey in one gulp.

Susan had always loved the big red dog. She remembered him as a puppy, and although she had been away in recent years and hadn't watched him grow up on the ranch, she still harbored an affection for him.

But what alarmed her most was her father and what rash action he might take. If he was convinced a wolf had killed Big Red, he might do something stupid. To Susan it was inconceivable that a wolf would come onto the ranch premises and deliberately attack the largest and most fearless dog they owned.

"Come on, Dad, a wolf isn't going to walk in here unprovoked and kill one of our dogs. That's ludicrous." She gave a nervous laugh.

"I guess you could say he was provoked, all right. We killed his mate and pups today." Rogers' voice was filled with irony.

"A wolf just isn't going to walk in here and attack our dogs, Dad. You know that," she repeated.

"What I know is what I saw out there," he snorted.

"Why don't you let the wildlife man that's coming out in the morning take care of it?" she suggested. When the colonel was distraught, he could be very unreasonable, and Susan knew she was probably wasting her breath.

"Those wolf lovers handle it? That's a laugh. They'll want to trap the SOB and turn him loose again down in Yellowstone." Everyone had heard about the wolf reintroduction program being implemented in Yellowstone National Park.

"That's what they're going to do with those damn pups, isn't it?" he demanded.

"I suppose so," Susan acknowledged, watching her father pour another shot of Scotch. "Please, Dad, you'll need to be up to par in the morning. You may find it wasn't a wolf after all. I just don't see how it could be."

Tossing the whiskey down in one swallow, he slammed the glass on the bar and stalked out of the room. "Don't worry about me. I'm going to be in fine shape in the morning. It's that damn lobo that better watch out," he growled with finality as he left.

A feeling of trepidation and unease settled over Susan. By now it was midnight. She had set her alarm clock for one o'clock in order to feed the three pups so she decided to stay up instead of going back to bed for an hour. She couldn't have slept anyhow.

Their formula was prepared and heated in fifteen minutes and she moved quickly to the barn before the milk got cold. She was surprised to find Pancho still there. He had finally gotten the dogs settled down and had been trying to calm the horses. They had become upset with the barking dogs and the new strange scent of the wolves which had invaded their domain of equine placidity.

"Since you are still up, Panch, maybe you can help me a moment," she said.

"Si, Missy, but I ain't feeding one of them squirmy devils. They'll take a hand clean off." Pancho was adamant and seeing the feeding bottles she was carrying filled him with a timorous anxiety. He had been amazed at the dexterity displayed by the young doctor in handling the growling pups, but he wanted no part of it.

"Don't worry. Nothing hazardous, Panch. Just help me move them up to the kitchen cellar after they've been fed. The dogs aren't going to stay quiet as long as these pups are in the barn and the horses aren't going to get any sleep either." The muffled shuffling of horses hooves in their stalls with an occasional kick attested to the correctness of Susan's assessment.

She had already gone into the empty stall where the young wolves were rustling about in the large washtub covered with a blanket. Without hesitation, she thrust her hand into the wiggling mass of fur and brought one out by the loose skin of its back. Whining and clawing, the young pup was soon eagerly nursing on the soft nipple, all animosity forgotten. Already he had become friendly with the soft rubber nipple so unlike the one he had become accustomed to on the warm belly of his mother. Susan quickly gave the same treatment to the other two babies. She and the old Mexican watched in fascination as the little round stomachs began to grow and become distended.

"The colonel ain't gonna like this, Missy," Pancho puffed as they moved awkwardly down the steep cellar stairwell after the feeding carrying the ancient washtub full of baby wolves. He had called her Missy since she was a little girl, and the fact that she was now an adult and a medical doctor didn't change the ingrained habit. It certainly wasn't a lack of respect for the young woman because Pancho loved her like a daughter. He would have followed her to purgatory, but he would not touch one of the menacing-looking fur balls.

The young animals were sleeping now, and Susan was counting on them being quiet for several hours. The colonel wouldn't hear them even if they did start up again. The Scotch whiskey always put him in a deep sleep and, besides, his hearing was almost nil without his hearing aids.

Susan was letting Pancho out the back door when it happened. It stopped them in their tracks. The plaintive howl of a gray wolf wafted down from the mountain to the north and seemed to settle over the ranch sky like an ominous cloak of retribution.

"Missy, you hear that?" Fear was in the question.

"Yeah, I heard it," she whispered, as a chill ran through her body.

The call came again; this time crescive, with more force and the eerie call hung in the air for an eternity.

Someone was coming, drawn by the kitchen light. It was Buck Dawson. He had not turned in after the excitement of the evening and had been outside the bunkhouse smoking a cigarette with a few of the other men when the wolf began to howl.

"That's the first wolf howl I've heard since I was a snot-nosed kid," he muttered, in a low voice. "Guess that tells us what killed old Red."

"Buck, I can't imagine a wolf coming in here like that and attacking Red. He had to walk right in front of the house. It's too . . . . . too unbelievable." Susan was searching for the right words to express her considerable doubts, although those doubts were now wavering with the portentous calls from the mountain.

Buck was a man who rarely jumped to conclusions, but he had a firm conviction in this case.

"It does sound a little far fetched, Miss Susan, but for the life of me I can't think of anything else it could have been." In deference to Susan's skepticism, Buck added, "Maybe we'll be able to learn more about what happened in the light of day. In the morning we'll get to the bottom of this."

There were two more long, lingering calls and then silence. The three people standing outside the back porch were also silent, each believing the others could hear the beating of their hearts. Susan felt the tingle of goose bumps on her body and realized she was suddenly very cold.

"We all need to get some sleep." she announced, as she turned to go inside. "It's been a long day for all of us."

When Dawson returned to the bunkhouse, he was surprised to find the cluster of men still standing outside. According to Ed Hastings, they had remained outside waiting to see if the mournful calls would resume. He would have been more truthful had he admitted they felt more comfortable as a group talking together and sharing the uneasiness.

Cody Watkins, the lead hunter that day was afflicted with a nervous prattle. "Maybe they's more'n one up there. That may be how they got old Red. Ganged up on him. Couldn'a done it no other way. Man, that dog was a horse." He couldn't stop talking. The bunkhouse gang had already decided it was the slain wolf's mate that had slipped into the dog lot and killed the big hound.

Watkins, despite his small, skinny frame had little fear of mortal man or beast. It was the unknown that unnerved him. His reddish, curly hair sticking out all around the oversized cowboy hat he always wore made him look like a girl in the face. But from the neck down he resembled an undernourished adolescent in his baggy clothes.

Brought up in a home environment that was rife with superstition and fear of the supernatural, the events of the night had stimulated his imagination to a frenzy. The idea that a wolf had crept into the dog lot and killed Big Red without so much as a cry of pain being emitted by the old dog was downright scary.

The spookiness that Watkins felt had spread to the other cowboys like loose water.

"Jesus, Buck," whispered Whit Whittaker, normally a hand that never spoke unless spoken to. "What do you make of it?"

"I ain't making nothing of it until morning," Buck answered. "Then we'll see."

Billy Greateyes had been sitting unnoticed on his three-legged stool nearby leaning back against the bunkhouse wall. Being unnoticed was always his cue to speak.

"The elders say the wolf is invisible. When the lone wolf howls, they become visible. They come from the south, the east, the west. Down from the mountains, through the trees, and across the rushing waters. Up from the prairies and the valleys. The lone wolf calls them to hunt, and they gather to go north.

"All the great antlered beasts hear the lone wolf's howl, and they shiver and shake. They know the wolves have become visible and will hunt them down." Even in the dark night the huge whites of Billy's eyes were shining like two white, unblinking marbles out of the blanket shrouding the Indian's face.

"I wish that old daft Indian was invisible," muttered Watkins nervously, feeling an involuntary shudder run through his body.

The Indian sage only stared into the black night as if hearing nothing.

"Well, you got to admit ain't nobody seen him," cackled Pecky Woodall, referring to the wolf.

"No, and ain't nobody gonna see him tonight," interjected Dawson. "It's getting dang cold out here. We best all hit the sack."

Suddenly, they were all feeling the cold, and there was an overpowering urge to get inside the bunkhouse. It was as if no one wanted to be left standing outside alone. In less than a minute only Billy Greateyes remained outside, sitting on his stool with the Indian blanket covering all but his face and the staring, circinate eyes that had given him his name.

He would remain thus until first light.

CHAPTER IV

Paul Taylor, as usual, was late getting back to the office. The U.S. Fish and Wildlife Service statistician had been in the field all day, and it had been a fifty mile drive back to Billings.

Martha McKay, his secretary, had already left the building but had put some messages on his desk. They were all routine except one. In her meticulous handwriting she had outlined a telephone call received at 4:05 PM from a Colonel Roland R. Rogers. Colonel Rogers had said a hunting party had killed a female wolf on Bear Mountain that morning. The wolf had five young and three were alive and in his possession. He wants us to come out and get them, and I told him someone would drive out to his ranch in the morning, she had written.

Taylor picked up the phone and dialed Martha McKay's number. They regularly received calls on misidentified animals, but this call was different. The man had said he had three live baby wolves. The wildlife biologist was extremely skeptical, but even if they weren't wolves, it would be necessary to make an identification and bring them in. Also, he was quite familiar with the Rogers name and reputation. Martha was right; someone would need to get out there first thing the next day.

"Hello," Martha answered in her pleasant, professional voice.

"Hi, Martha, it's me. Sorry I was late getting back. Hate to call you at home but just read your note on Colonel Rogers' call."

"No problem, Paul. Alex hasn't gotten home yet, and I'm just sitting here thinking about what to fix for supper."

Martha McKay was an attractive brunette hovering on the brink of middle age. Without vanity, she made no effort to color the dreaded gray that had sprung forth in her dark hair. She was beginning to appear matronly, but it was apparent that she had been a trim, lovely woman in her youth.

Martha and Alex McKay had six children, all grown and on their own or away in college. She had worked for Fish and Wildlife for fifteen years, the last eight as Paul Taylor's secretary. She had enormous respect and admiration for the thirty-five year old biologist gained through years of close professional association with him.

Five years earlier, Taylor had lost his young wife, Carolyn. She had been killed instantly in an automobile crash. The shock had never left the man, and Martha McKay was convinced it had changed him forever. He had abandoned every aspect of his previous life and now had no interest whatsoever in anything but his work.

Paul Taylor had shown no sign of snapping out of his deep grief, and Martha had done everything she could to help him. Even to the extent about two years earlier of arranging a date between him and her visiting niece from

Portland. The young woman was a knockout and eager to meet the tall, handsome Taylor, especially after Martha had heaped her considerable praises for the wildlife official on her.

The meeting and subsequent evening had been a disaster.

Getting Paul Taylor back in the land of the living had been Martha's secret project, although to the office force it had not been so secret. Now, after five years she was ready to give up. Abandon the entire effort. After all, the man had to cooperate if there was to be any progress at all.

And cooperate he hadn't. Personnel get-togethers, picnics, civic invitations, church functions; you name it, he hadn't bothered. Office parties were out of the question, but Martha couldn't fault him for that. She didn't care for them either.

It certainly hadn't been Paul Taylor's lack of physical attributes that had ruined the evening for her niece. Over six feet tall with the build of a football player, the man was the epitome of young manhood. His broad chest, narrow hips and flat stomach had turned many a female eye.

The full mane of dark hair, dark eyebrows, and liquid brown eyes gave an Adonis look to his finely chiseled face. Had he been so inclined he probably could have had his pick of eligible Billings girls. The death of his wife, however, had removed all thought of the opposite sex from his mind. After five years it appeared he would shun the ladies forever. Carolyn Taylor had consumed him, and it looked like she would not spit him out until his final breath on earth.

Whether it was the grief that would not go away or some permanent psychological damage to his mind, the fact remained that Paul Taylor's life had been compromised indefinitely.

Due to being privy to all the correspondence that moved through the Billings office, Martha was familiar with the pressure that had been exerted to move Taylor to Washington. Taylor's capabilities were well known throughout the agency, and efforts had been under way for a long time to persuade him to transfer to national headquarters. Being FWS's top field statistician was as far as he was going to go if he didn't make the move, and Taylor was quite aware of that.

Yet, he couldn't stand the thought of a permanent desk job. He enjoyed the field too much and that is where he spent most of his time. Even to the point of neglecting his office duties. It was why he spent so much after-hours time as well as every Saturday morning in the office. It was the privacy he enjoyed. Being by himself. There were no distractions and he could concentrate. Get things done.

The powers-that-be must never have experienced a stint in the western field. Could money be that important? To consider pushing a pencil inside the D.C. beltway after participating in the stewardship of the most diverse wild ungulate population in the entire lower forty-eight states was ridiculous. Actually, it was laughable.

Did those people in Washington realize that he was keeping track of the sum total of more ungulate animals than any other U.S. Fish and Wildlife official across the United States? He had gone to college to learn how to manage wildlife, not people. A move to Washington would mean personnel management.

Oh well, it was his choice, thank goodness. Why worry about it.

"I think I'll go out to the Rogers ranch personally in

the morning. I'll go early so I should be back in the office before noon," Taylor advised. The next day was Friday, and he wanted to get his desk cleared before the all-week conference in Helena scheduled for the following week. Martha knew what Paul meant by early; before daylight probably. "Why don't you send Roy out there? It's over eighty miles from here, Paul. You'll kill your whole day," she urged.

Martha was so thorough. Clearly she had consulted a map and had already decided how the assignment should be handled. Paul smiled as she talked. She was constantly telling him how to run things, but he really didn't mind. It was always done out of concern for him, and the intent was innocent enough.

Roy Mason was a young biologist who had joined the local staff recently, and it would be a good public relations experience for him. If Mason was going to get his feet wet, this was a perfect initial task for him. But something about Colonel Rogers' phone call told Taylor that it might be best for him to make the trip. The call had been about wolves which was far from routine.

"Martha, I have a gut feeling about this. Don't ask me why. Ordinarily, I would discount most people's contention of finding gray wolf pups, especially in the vicinity of the Rogers ranch, but this man should know what he is talking about. Rogers is one of the biggest cattle ranchers in the state and has been in operation as long as I can remember. I'll probably find coyotes, but you never know.

"Roy's just getting his feet on the ground around here. I'm not saying he can't handle this, but I think I should be the one to go." Paul hoped he was sounding convincing.

"If Colonel Rogers is that knowledgeable, he should

know that gray wolves are an endangered species," Martha pointed out acidly.

"Maybe he does. Wolves showing up in the area around Rogers Ranch don't enjoy the full protection of the Endangered Species Act. At least he has reported it, so he must be a man of integrity. This is probably not a case of wanton killing."

"OK, you win," she said, with a sigh of resignation. "I'll see you tomorrow."

"Thanks, Martha. I'll get back as soon as I can."

"By the way," she said, as if suddenly remembering. "That reporter that's been popping in and out of the office for the last two weeks blew in, blew off, and blew out again this morning. He wants to talk to you. Thinks you are avoiding him." Years of receiving the public had given Martha a unique insight into human behavior. From polite to rude, meek to overbearing, she had met them all. Time and her front-line position in the office had dulled her perspective toward people, but she continued a valiant effort to mask her indifference and cynicism.

Paul laughed. "Don't worry. Those people are persistent. He'll find me sooner or later."

The Wolf Recovery Program had created a media outburst in Montana, Idaho, and Wyoming. Hardly a day went by that some article wasn't in the newspapers about wolves being released in Yellowstone National Park by Fish and Wildlife. The releases in central Idaho were also reported although they produced a little less public volatility. The release program had been quite controversial which was the ingredient to make it newsworthy.

When the program had been implemented in Yellowstone, there had been concern that a few wolves might stray or wander outside the park boundaries. But Yellowstone would be almost two hundred miles from the Rogers ranch. Very unlikely a Yellowstone wolf would travel that distance or in that direction. These thoughts were going through Taylor's mind as he hung up the phone slowly.

Still, what if Rogers did know what he was talking about? There had not been gray wolves reported in that section of the state in over fifty years. Maybe longer.

Could it be possible? he speculated as he turned off the office lights.

****

Taylor left his apartment at six o'clock the next morning stopping at the office for about ten minutes to leave a couple of notes for Martha. Then he stopped at a McDonald's for a sausage biscuit and coffee at the drive-through window. He wanted to get to the Rogers ranch around eight o'clock, which was as early as he could respectfully come calling in his own mind. They might be late risers as his perception of the affluent told him. It shouldn't take long to pick up the young animals, whatever they might be, and be back in the office well before noon.

He had checked the map and determined that Rogers Ranch was in the vicinity of the Snowy Mountains. Certainly not an area where one would normally expect to find wolves. Remote enough up there but just not wolf country.

As he drove north, the traffic thinned and then became almost non-existent. Electing to play it safe, he went by way of Roundup via Route 87, then crossed over on Route 297 leading toward the Snowy Mountains. Trying to take a shortcut up Route 3 might have been unwise since he didn't know exactly where Rogers Ranch was located. The directions Rogers had given Martha were explicit enough, but he didn't want to miss the turnoff at the ranch road.

The turn toward the Snowy Mountains exposed the magnificence of a Montana Big Sky spring day. The cold front that had rushed through during the night had cleared the clouds, and the blue of the sky was breathtaking. The frontal passage had left a numbing cold which seemed to add to the brisk clarity of the beautiful April morning.

The rangeland was greening up and splashes of pink, white, yellow, and purple flowers dotted the landscape as if an artist had slung a dripping brush in exasperation at the largest canvas in the world. The wild grasses rolled in the light breeze like a landlocked ocean, and if the sight of it didn't stir the senses, the clean fragrance did.

It was springtime, and out of the rock crevices, fissures and cracks sprang the Montana myriad of early flower blossoms, low and creeping until the ground was a multifaceted blanket of color. The asters, bitterroot, daisies, and primrose were competing for dominance and seeking space in which to grow.

It was the time of the famed Montana "pink snows" when the tiny plants thrust their lovely profusion upward to give a spectacular hue to the late spring snows. It was the kind of day that had endeared Paul Taylor to this strikingly beautiful land.

Ordinarily, Taylor was always planning and thinking ahead when he had occasion for these long drives through the Montana countryside, but this Friday morning he allowed himself to reminisce. The day was too lovely to be in deep technical thought.

For some reason he was thinking about his early

childhood on the Wisconsin farm where he grew up. He was remembering his first real friend.

The school bus had stopped to let him out, and he was walking up the narrow farm lane that led to his house a quarter mile away. It had been a spring day very similar to the one he was now enjoying. Perhaps that was why he was now remembering it so vividly.

His father had been out in the yard talking to a man in a green uniform, and Paul's curiosity had been overwhelming. Rarely would he have imposed himself uninvited among his elders but he couldn't walk past the two men without lingering. About ten feet away he paused, not wanting to interrupt their conversation but desperately wanting to hear what they were saying.

"We'll keep an eye peeled, Sam, and anything we see that's the least bit suspicious-looking, we'll let you know." Charles Taylor was ending his discussion with the Wisconsin conservation officer. It seemed that some deer poaching had been going on in the area. Spotlighting, as it was called locally.

Like osmosis, Paul had drawn near. So close that both men had turned to look at him.

"This is my son, Paul, Mr. Howell. Anything goes on in the woods around here, Paul ought to know about it. Spends most of his time there. And running up and down Ferrel Creek." The elder Taylor turned to go in the house, and Sam Howell, who had given him a perfunctory nod, had begun walking toward his car.

"Mister, want to see an eagle?" The words had popped out of the young mouth without thought. He had kept the secret of the bald eagle bottled up inside him for over a month, afraid to tell anyone. The secret had become so burdensome that he couldn't repress it any longer, and this was the perfect person with whom to share it.

The officer had stopped and turned around, a patronizing expression on his face. He was old for a conservation officer. With a heavy, reddish beard interspersed with gray, he looked scraggly. The watery, gray eyes and ruddy cheeks signaled daily exposure to the elements. If he had removed the stiff, official hat, Paul would have seen that he was completely bald.

"Sure it's an eagle, son? Lots of red-tails around here," he questioned good naturedly.

"Yes sir. It's a bald eagle. It's got a white head," Paul had answered confidently.

"Well, it's late and I need to get back in before the office closes."

The indecision had been noted, and Paul saw his opening.

"Won't take no time. You won't even have to cross the crick." He had already sprinted to the farm house.

Howell had no time to protest nor long to wait. The door had quickly burst open again, and the young boy ran out pulling a ragged sweat shirt over his head. He had also changed his trousers and shoes and carried a wrinkled brown paper sack in one hand. He wanted to get away fast before his father caught him and demanded that he clean the milk room before heading for the woods.

Cleaning the milk room had been his job for over a year although he was only ten years old. As long as he kept the milkers clean and shiny and the floor scrubbed clean, his dad didn't mind his daily wanderings to his favorite haunts. He even washed the milk room windows once a week which was far more often than the windows got washed in the house.

Paul led a blistering pace across the north pasture toward Ferrel Creek, and Sam Howell had to rein him in before they had gone a hundred yards.

"Whoa, boy. You want me to see this eagle, you gonna have to slow down."

"Sorry. Can you make it to those woods?" Paul was pointing to a mature wood lot in the distance. The lot was square and Ferrel Creek paralleled the south edge. At the southwestern corner, the creek made a ninety degree turn to the north and followed the boundary of timber to its northwestern corner. The creek then meandered away from the woods through the rolling farmland, finally emptying into the Little Rib River about three miles away.

When they got to the bend in the creek, Paul slowed and began whispering.

"He's in a big sugar maple right around the crook of the crick," he confided.

As they rounded the bend, Howell saw the large maple growing near the creek bank about fifty yards away. The tree was old and twisted with half its branches decayed, the dead stubs projecting grotesquely among the live ones. The spring leaf expansion had just started, giving the tree a thin, weak look. In the very top sat a very large mature bald eagle, its piercing eyes focused intently on the two intruders. The small dead limb on which it was perched was miraculously supporting the weight of the giant raptor.

"You better stay here," whispered Paul. "He's not used to nobody but me."

The young boy stepped out of his shoes, slipped into the knee deep water and waded to the other side. Howell knew the creek waters were icy cold this early in the spring and noted the youngster didn't seem to notice it at all.

Slowly, Paul walked to the base of the gnarled old tree, unfolded the paper bag, and dropped something on the ground. The eagle hadn't stirred, and Sam Howell realized he was watching an event the likes of which he had never seen in forty years of wildlife work.

The lad walked slowly back and waded back across the creek.

"What did you put under the tree?" Howell asked in a low voice.

"Meat scraps. I do this about twice a week or as often as I can collect enough meat for him. He likes fish the most." Paul was proud of himself. "I figure he might bring a mate if I feed him. They could build a nest in the woods where nobody would bother them."

They watched the giant bird awhile longer.

"He won't come down for the meat 'til we're gone," Paul offered, not wanting to rush the conservation officer but at the same time wanting to let the hungry eagle get to its food.

The two had walked back to the officer's car in silence. Sam Howell had opened the car door, and Paul had the sinking feeling that the burly old man was going to drive away without a word. He had been so proud of himself he was ready to burst. Surely the officer would say something. Some comment on being shown a bald eagle should have been appropriate, especially from a real wildlife officer.

Instead of getting in the car, however, Howell had reached in and retrieved a green-backed logbook.

"How old are you, son?" he had asked, turning back to the boy.

"Ten."

"Would you like to do a little survey work for me? It would just be for me and not the department. Because of your age, you know."

The glow of Paul's eyes gave him his answer.

"Fill in the information as outlined in this log. Birds, fish, animals; whatever you might see. After school, Saturdays. Whatever time you can give me. I can't pay much but it'll give you a little spending money." Sam was touched as he saw the expression of ecstasy in the young lad's face.

"I'll come out about once a week. After you've gotten home from school. See what you've got."

It was the most exciting event of Paul Taylor's youth, and he had surprised Sam Howell with his enthusiasm and dedication to his new job.

One Saturday he was investigating some beaver dams far from home and realized he was approaching the mouth of Ferrel Creek where it emptied into the Little Rib. He remembered hearing about the broad swamp land where the creek flowed into the river so he decided to investigate. No one ever went there because it was so wet and soggy. In later years it would become known as wetlands, and instead of it being regarded as useless swamp, it would gain distinct and valuable status as excellent wildlife habitat. Particularly for migratory birds as Paul would find out as he forged ahead toward the distant river.

The swamp began to be Paul's favorite place to visit on Saturdays, and it allowed him to fatten his reports to Sam. The place was hard to get to without getting wet feet, and few people paid attention to it or visited there in those days. Paul had found a slight rise on the south side of the shallow body of water where he could draw near without being seen. That is, if he got on his hands and knees and was willing to suffer the wrath of his mother when he got home, wet and cold.

Wood ducks, shovelers, teals, mergansers, mallards, black ducks. Loons and grebes. Vast flocks of Canada geese. He would stay up late into every Saturday night wrestling with identification of the day's sightings. Sam had given him an old Peterson bird book that he had practically devoured.

One fall day he casually asked Sam, who had been delighted with Paul's weekly reports, if he would like to see some white geese. Sam had looked at him with a jaundiced eye but had said nothing.

"We can go on Saturday. They might still be there," Paul had said hopefully.

"OK," Sam had replied. Curiosity overcame him because the boy had become so reliable.

In the beginning Sam had regretted the decision. They had driven as close as possible to the south end of the swamp, and he had gotten wet crawling up the shallow rise that gave them cover only so long as they stayed low to the ground. For Sam that meant on his belly.

Finally, they had been able to peer over the hillock and see the wide expanse of marsh water. Sam had immediately forgotten about his discomfort and wet clothes. About a dozen majestic white waterfowl were clutched together not thirty yards from them.

Sam's voice had been a whispered croak. "Boy, those aren't white geese. Those are swans. Tundra swans. Used to be named whistlers. Whistling swans." The old wildlifer had been so excited his low voice shook.

They had lain in the wet grass for over an hour watching the bobbing beauties feed, until they both were so cold they were forced to retreat.

Now, twenty-five years later, Paul was remembering it like it was yesterday.

Over time, the two had shared a myriad of bird and animal sightings and in the process had become fast friends. The best of friends as Paul remembered.

The eagle had brought a mate the following year, and Paul and Sam had kept that sacred secret until the fateful day when Paul was a senior in high school. Again, he had been walking up the farm lane after getting off the school bus. His father had stood waiting for him in the yard. Obviously, something was amiss. Charles Taylor would never waste time waiting for his son to arrive from school.

"Thought I should catch you before you got in the house, Son." The elder Taylor had a stricken look on his face.

"What's happened, Dad?" Paul questioned, alarm running through his body.

"Sam died this morning. They think it was a heart attack."

The whole family had gone to the funeral. It was the first funeral of someone he loved that he had ever attended. It was the saddest occasion of Paul Taylor's young life, and the first time he had ever cried for another human being.

Oh, he had cried before, all right. He had cried for the doe deer he had found beside the road with two broken legs. Suffering with an agony apparent only in her eyes.

And when their golden retriever, Rusty, had died it had broken his heart, and his crying had been done in the privacy of the milk room.

He had cried when Algonquin High had lost the very first game in the State Regional basketball playoffs during his senior year. He had played guard but not well enough. It had been a bitter setback.

But that kind of crying was nothing compared to losing Sam Howell to death. The hero-worship for Sam was the strongest emotion he had ever felt. What Paul didn't understand at the time was the enrichment and inspiration the relationship had brought to him and which would be with him the rest of his days. He only knew he wanted to grow up and be like Sam Howell.

Getting a scholarship at the University of Wisconsin at Madison and majoring in wildlife conservation, he worked at it until he had received a B.S. degree and then a Masters degree. After making application for a position with the U.S. Fish and Wildlife Service, Paul discovered the high regard in which Sam Howell had held him. The letter of recommendation from the Wisconsin Department of Natural Resources that accompanied his application had stated that they had never been privileged to recommend a more meritorious university graduate. Somehow, the recommendation had Sam Howell written all over it.

The most exciting event of Paul Taylor's adult life, discounting his ecstatic marriage to Carolyn Smith, was becoming special statistician of the crown jewel of all the U.S. Fish and Wildlife Regions in the United States — the Mountain - Prairie Region. Even though Gladys Johnson, his high school English teacher, had taught him never to end a sentence with a preposition, it was where it was at.

The widest variety of wild ungulates in the lower forty-eight states and an economy largely dependent on wildlife. Pronghorn, mountain goat, moose, elk, bighorn sheep. American bison, deer, both mule and white-tail. Just name it and it could be found in this magnificent wild land.

The only remaining grizzly bear population in the

conterminous United States. The most prized inland game fishing in America. Even wolves, which were precipitating his trip today. A hunting and fishing bonanza unequaled anywhere else in the country.

And, of course, that part of the National Wildlife Refuge System that he took professional responsibility for in maintaining the nation's western wildlife heritage. He had gravitated to statistics honestly enough. It went back to the first day he had met Sam Howell, and Sam had retrieved the green logbook from his car and given him his first job. He had been ten years old.

The icing on the cake had been Carolyn whom he had met and courted at the university. They had married after his job was assured at FWS. She would have followed him to the ends of the earth, and when the transfer to Billings, Montana came through, it had actually seemed like the ends of the earth.

But she hadn't objected and, in fact, had relished the move. The harsh weather and vast land had required adjustment for both Carolyn and Paul, but Montana's beauty had grown on them. And grown and grown. It never got old until that devastating November day. It had been over five years ago, and Paul still was incapable of dealing with it. One day a vibrant, beautiful, smart, sensitive and loving woman. The next a corpse in a closed casket so no one could see the horror of her final seconds. So completely senseless and worst of all, a drunken driver.

At least after five years he had learned how to turn off the thoughts. He just hadn't learned how to turn on new ones.

In the distance he could see Old Baldy and it brought him back to the present. The turn off to the Rogers ranch was close. There would be several miles of private road to travel.

Getting his thoughts back to the purpose of his trip, he wondered what kind of man he would be meeting. Colonel Roland R. Rogers. Modern day cattle baron. Well, in his line of work he had met all kinds.

Taylor did not believe he would be surprised.

CHAPTER V

It was exactly eight o'clock when Taylor drove into the parking area of Rogers Ranch. It had been a long trip for only eighty miles. Especially in Montana where speed was regarded as part of Montanan freedom. However, the last ten miles had been rocky and slow.

The road into the ranch was certainly no indication of the kind of facility he would find. He had heard of the Rogers ranch for years but never had occasion to visit the place.

First, the two tall stone pillars marking the ranch entrance were startling considering the rural setting. No gate or fence suggesting a boundary. Just the slender columns standing guard like soldiers at Buckingham Palace. No ornate identification. Only a small, bronze plaque on each structure displaying the words Rogers Ranch.

Then the pea gravel driveway for half a mile, raked and smoothed as precisely as the manicured lawn around the house. The professionally landscaped premises. The gray, slate roof and massive granite steps leading into the impressive dwelling.

The sprawling stone residence indicated conspicuous wealth, and the long, fancy-roofed barn nearby belied the fact that the complex was a cattle ranch. If he hadn't known otherwise, he would have guessed it was a quarter horse ranch. Looking at his watch before mounting the stone steps to the front door, he hoped he wasn't too early for these people. They might be late risers. He was almost intimidated by the colossus of the place. So much so that he chose to meekly peck on the imposing red door rather than use the ornate brass knocker.

And then it happened. Seemingly, before he had finished knocking, the door sprang open and the most beautiful woman he had ever seen in his life stood there smiling up at him. Taylor found himself practically incapable of speaking. She was a sparkling blonde with such clear, blue eyes they seemed to threaten his equilibrium. The radiance of her smile was so overwhelming that he could only smile back foolishly. Suddenly, he had been diminished to a school kid who had just discovered girls. His legs had turned to jelly, and his voice, once he found it, sounded strange and wavy.

"Good morning. I'm Paul Taylor with Fish and Wildlife," he finally choked out.

"Of course. Come in," she offered, standing back and letting the door swing open all the way. The tall, dark-haired man had not been what Susan had expected. Dressed in khaki pants and cowboy boots with only a thin, white shirt open at the collar, she had anticipated a uniform of some kind. There was no hat or jacket although the cold morning air created by the fast moving cold front was bone chilling.

"Dad told me he had called you. My name is Susan Rogers," she said, extending her hand as he walked through the door.

"Good to meet you," he exclaimed, her small, soft hand sending a shiver through his body. "Hope I'm not too early," he continued, noting it was a stupid thing to say. "Not at all," she answered, as she turned to lead him through a long hallway toward the rear of the house. "We're having coffee in the kitchen. Your timing is perfect."

Her simple, unassuming manner helped Taylor relax a bit, but this woman was quality and he was not going to be completely at ease in such a privileged environment.

"I left my coat in the car. Didn't realize it had gotten so cold." He couldn't control his mouth.

"Yes. I understand it may cloud up and snow later today," she answered.

As they walked deeper into the spacious structure, she asked, "Did you drive all the way from Billings this morning?"

"I'm an early riser," he laughed. Another stupid remark, he chastised himself.

She turned through a doorway, and Taylor found himself in a huge kitchen. The cathedral ceiling was supported by the most massive timbers Taylor had ever seen. Polished and shining, he wondered who did the dusting. The room was larger than his entire duplex apartment.

A rectangular table of immense proportions was in the center of the room. A lone figure sat at the far end hunkered over a cup of coffee. The table could have seated twenty people, but only ten or twelve straight-backed chairs were scattered around its sides in no particular order.

A round, middle-aged lady who appeared to be of Mexican descent was at the kitchen sink washing dishes. The Rogers family apparently had just finished breakfast. The only other thing that immediately caught Taylor's eye was the gigantic fireplace along the outside wall. The large stones reminded him of the huge steps at the front of the house. He had never seen cut stones of such size.

The active fireplace looked as if it had seen a lot of usage and was blackened and charred. Utensils of every description hanging from the mantle made it look like a rustic, stone cornucopia of cookware. The fire was rather anemic-looking considering the size of the long grate, yet the room was warm and comfortable despite its cavernous depth.

The young woman led Taylor to the end of the long table where the old man waited.

"Mr. Taylor, this is my father, Colonel Rogers. Dad, this is Paul Taylor from the U.S. Fish and Wildlife Service. He may be who you talked to yesterday."

Paul noted her cultured voice was precise right down to the correct name of his agency.

The colonel didn't attempt to rise but did shake Taylor's hand laconically when it was extended to him.

"And this is Rozita," Susan continued lightly.

Taylor and Rozita mumbled greetings.

"No, I talked to a woman. Did she tell you about the wolves?" Colonel Rogers' voice was gruff, almost without civility.

"Sit down, Mr. Taylor," Susan interrupted. "Do you want cream or sugar?" She had already put an empty cup in front of him and was retrieving the coffee pot from the stove.

"Black will be fine," he answered, sitting down. "Yes, Colonel, my secretary told me what you told her."

Colonel Rogers wasn't going to beat around the bush with niceties. "Mr. Taylor, last night a damn lobo wolf came down off the mountain and killed my best dog. We figure he was the female's mate. I can tell you, sir, he's dead meat."

The colonel had raised his voice, and the defiant look in his eyes bored into Taylor.

The wildlife biologist's face reflected surprise and shock. What he was hearing didn't make any sense whatsoever.

"What actually happened, Colonel?" he asked.

"The son of a bitch slipped into the dog lot and killed my best dog; that's what actually happened," the colonel repeated heatedly. He had been out earlier trying to determine what had caused the death of Big Red. Both he and Buck Dawson had concluded it was the wolf that had howled later from the mountain.

Susan saw her father was going to get worked up so she attempted to defuse the situation. "Mr. Taylor, let me take you down to the dog lot. Buck Dawson, our foreman, is down there looking for tracks now. He can fill you in on everything."

Taylor thought it would be better not to say anything further to Colonel Rogers who was now becoming quite agitated. He needed more information on what had happened, and he wanted to see the young pups to make sure he was dealing with wolves here.

Rising to his feet, he said, "Good idea. Lead the way."

Going through the back door, they headed toward the long, fancy barn. As they walked along a flagstone walk, Paul was able to see more of the ranch buildings behind the barn. These people were far from ordinary cattle ranchers.

"Where are the pups?" he asked as they walked.

"Actually, they are in the cellar under the kitchen. Dad thinks they are in the barn, but I brought them in last night after their one o'clock feeding. I fed them early this morning while Dad was out investigating Big Red's death, and they went to sleep. I was scared they would wake up and start yowling while we were having breakfast," she said, giggling impulsively. "Dad would really have a conniption if he knew they were in the house."

"I need to see them for a positive identification," the wildlife official said. The woman's laughter had gone straight to his heart and his head was in a twirl.

"Don't worry, they're wolves all right. If Buck Dawson says they are, they are."

A big, burly cowboy came around the end of the barn toward them. Doffing his hat politely, he asked, "Did I hear my name mentioned?"

"Buck, this is Paul Taylor from the Fish and Wildlife Service. He's going to take the orphans."

The two men shook hands vigorously, and Taylor decided he liked the grizzled old cowhand. No nonsense here, he thought.

Pancho had already removed the red dog from the lot to bury him in the pet cemetery at the east end of the ranch. There was no evidence of a fight or struggle at the site of the killing. Just bare, hard ground which looked like all the rest of the dog lot. No blood or patches of hair were present although there were some scratches in the hard ground where Big Red had lived his final moments.

It took Dawson several minutes to relate the entire account of the wolf episode including the hunt and subsequent attack on the big hound. His low, rambling voice drawled out the story in slow detail. He didn't include his doubts that the dogie kill had been made by a wolf. Dawson knew it had been a cougar, but he didn't say in deference to his boss.

"No tracks, the ground is too hard here in the dog lot, but it had to the lobo. A bear would have left claw marks on the dog and hair all around. A mountain lion too but they are far too timid to attack a dog unprovoked," Dawson finally summarized.

"But if there was no physical evidence of a wolf being present how can you be sure it was a wolf?" Taylor asked. He still wasn't convinced.

"What else could have gotten to Big Red's throat? His windpipe was cut almost in two. Besides, there was evidence," Buck confided. "Last night about an hour or two after it happened we heard him howling. Up on Bear Mountain. Miss Susan, Pancho, and myself were standing in the yard. The men heard it too. I haven't heard a wolf howl since I was small enough for fish bait, Mr. Taylor, but we heard one last night."

Taylor didn't want to start an argument with this man whom he had just met and who obviously had a lot of Montana savy, but he couldn't accept what he was hearing.

"Yes, but that doesn't mean it was the same animal that killed the dog," he insisted rather emphatically.

Dawson shrugged. "Maybe, maybe not. It's just my belief."

This man is no off-the-wall neophyte, thought Taylor. His words and opinions have credence. But what he was saying was so preposterous it defied belief. It was the most baffling wildlife story Paul Taylor had ever heard.

"Look, Taylor," interjected Susan. "Dad's probably in his study by now. Let's go to the cellar and you can see the babies." Taylor didn't believe a wolf had killed Big Red and neither did she. It was best to try to head off any difference of opinion before an all out argument developed.

Taylor was glad for the impasse because he had run out of questions. He didn't want to get in an argument either.

When they returned to the kitchen, the old man was missing, and Rozita was still at the sink keeping busy.

"Good," Susan said, with noticeable relief. "Dad's gone to his study."

She led the way down the steep and narrow cellar steps and turned on an anemic overhead light. Removing a light cover stretched across an old washtub, the bodies of the three baby wolves became visible. Taylor was stunned. There was no question of their identity.

"Man, they're wolves all right," he uttered in a whisper.

The sudden light had disturbed the sleeping youngsters, and they had begun to stir and whimper. Taylor attempted to spread the legs of one to determine its gender, and when it made a sudden defensive move he jerked his hand back. Quickly, Susan reached in and pulled the pup out into her lap.

"There are two males and one female," she remarked. "I thought you were a wildlife expert," she added, a little crossly.

Embarrassment flowed all over him. Susan was conscious of it so she changed the subject. She really hadn't meant to sound so knowingly astute.

"How old do you think they are?" she whispered. They had been whispering for no apparent reason.

"Maybe three, four weeks," he speculated. He couldn't believe how adept she was at handling the surly little babies.

"Yeah, I figure that's about right," she offered in agreement.

She was so close as they knelt together over the

galvanized tub that he could feel her presence against him. The clean, heady smell of her fired his senses and concentrating on the young wolves was difficult. This woman was doing strange things to his heart, and he couldn't understand it.

"You seem to know a lot about young animals," he stammered.

"I should. I've raised enough of them. No wolves yet but just about everything else." She shifted her weight and her shoulder pressed against his own. She didn't attempt to pull away. They watched the wiggling youngsters silently for awhile.

"What will you do with them?" she asked, somewhat accusingly.

"Take them in to Doc Ferguson's clinic first," he replied. "He'll check them over and keep them until they are weaned. Give them their shots, worm them, etc. From there they probably will go down to Yellowstone to be introduced into Wolfman White's program."

Doctor Wallace Ferguson had been the Rogers ranch veterinarian for as far back as Susan could remember, and she trusted him like another father. But she wasn't so sure of the rest of Taylor's answer.

"Who's Wolfman White?" she wanted to know.

"He's our wolf specialist up in Helena," Taylor said with a soft chuckle. "He is implementing the Wolf Recovery Program in Yellowstone. It's part of restoring the park ecosystem to its natural state."

Susan knew about the wolf recovery plan for Yellowstone. Almost daily there had been articles about it in the Billings *Gazette*. She also knew the program was very controversial with many factions, mostly cattle and sheep ranchers, being against it.

"Think it will work?" she asked.

"Who knows? It might if the main predator doesn't become an overriding factor."

"Your mean hunters?"

"Yeah. At least a lot will be learned from the program." Taylor found himself enjoying talking to this young woman who was softly pressing against him. He wondered if she was doing it on purpose or was unaware of the contact.

"They will be too young to turn loose in the wild," she noted logically.

"Oh, Wolfman will keep them isolated until next spring. They are never released under a year old and usually in the spring. Getting established in a pack well before cold weather is essential for their survival."

"I love the little female. She's going to be almost white," Susan remarked tenderly. She turned her head toward his only inches away, the blue of her eyes melting his heart.

"Could I keep the female until time to release her? I'm sure I could do as good a job raising her as your people." Her voice was beseeching, bordering on pleading but also a little accusatory.

"Ms. Rogers, it's against the law for private citizens to be in possession of live wild animals." He had made another *faux pas* as he remembered hearing she was a doctor. Starting to continue, she interrupted him.

"But I could get a permit." She was eager now, urging him with her eyes to say yes. "Doc Ferguson will vouch for me. He'll probably want my milk formula since I have them eating so well."

"I'm sorry, but standard permits aren't issued for

endangered species animals. I'm sure you would do a splendid job of raising the pup, but it's something best left to the experts."

"Experts! I've raised more wild animals than all your "experts" put together." She had broken their spell of whispering closeness and bounced to her feet. Turning to him she locked his eyes again, this time with a hard, steely glare. "It's just government bureaucracy, and I think you know it, Taylor. Come on, I'll help you take them to your car." She was already covering the washtub that was getting increasingly noisy.

"They'll need to be fed again shortly. You better get them on to Doc Ferguson's," she said icily.

Taylor was silent as they moved the tub full of baby wolves to the tailgate of his Bronco. The silence became awkward as he prepared to leave. Susan had become quiet and distant and seemed ready to let him leave without another word.

Pondering what to say, he spent some time putting on the jacket he had left in the vehicle. He couldn't just drive off. It was too final. The brief relationship would be ended, and it would be all his fault. Unexpectedly, it popped out of his mouth without any conscious thought. Only adhesive tape over his lips could have prevented it.

"Look, I'll talk to Wolfman. Maybe he would be willing to issue a special dispensation in your case. I can't promise you, though."

The look that came over Susan's face melted his heart. It was a mixture of astonishment and great joy.

"Taylor, you won't regret it. I promise."

He wanted to kick himself, but the words had been said. He could see how important it was to her to keep the female pup. It wasn't a whim at all but a genuine commitment for the welfare of the animal.

"Don't get your hopes up," he mumbled, realizing he had really stuck his neck out.

"Can you wait until I fix their formula? We can feed them on the way into town. I need to get my purse and a few things." She was bounding toward the house, and all Taylor could do was follow, her excitement obvious in her rush.

"But I can't bring you back," he called in exasperation.

She slowed down allowing him to catch up. "That's OK. This is Friday and Pancho goes to town every Friday for supplies and the mail. He'll bring me back. In fact, most Fridays I go in with him. Gives me a chance to do a little shopping, get my hair done, you know, get away." The woman seemed to be walking on a cloud, and Taylor wondered what he had gotten himself into.

It hadn't taken long. Pancho was getting ready to leave for Billings and she had a word with him. She certainly wasn't like most women. In ten minutes she was ready and looked like a million dollars. Still in jeans, sweater and jacket but her face was out of Vogue magazine.

In addition to that she had found the time to fix the wolves' bottles and tell everybody she was leaving. The woman was organized beyond belief.

While he waited, as brief as it was, he analyzed his off-the-wall response to her request. Regardless of how he thought about it, there was no getting around the fact that he had caved in to her imploring entreaty because he desperately wanted to see her again. He couldn't simply take the tub full of baby gray wolves and remove himself from her presence forever.

An excitement was evident in her demeanor as she scurried around preparing to leave and Paul had the dreadful thought that he had gone too far in raising her expectations of keeping the young wolf. If Wolfman didn't approve the arrangement it would be a crushing disappointment for her and she would blame him.

Unfortunately, he was completely helpless in the matter. For the first time in his life he found himself incapable of saying the word no.

CHAPTER VI

The drive to Billings was made mostly in silence. They seemed to be quietly evaluating each other, neither prone to talk much.

Susan had fed the baby wolves one by one in her lap after moving the washtub up close to her seat where she could reach them. Taylor was occupied with formulating the words for the disagreeable task of lecturing her. Her father had killed an endangered species animal, and it could not be ignored.

Paul was impressed with the way she handled the sharp-toothed little monsters. He was also bewildered at the emotional impact the young blond goddess was having on him. Women had held little interest for him since the death of Carolyn five years earlier, and he couldn't understand it. This lady was turning him all mushy every time she looked at him, and he couldn't muster any control over what he was saying. What did come out of his mouth reminded him of a stammering idiot.

His furtive glances at her hands had made him feel

uncomfortable. No wedding band or diamond ring. Why had he checked that out? So completely unlike him. It was all so crazy. And hopeless. Susan Rogers was so far beyond his league he wasn't even in the ball park. Socially, economically, intellectually. It was not only hopeless but absurd.

He had heard she was a doctor who had given up her position in a large hospital back East to return to the family cattle ranch. Presumably, to run the ranch for her elderly father after the death of her mother. It had been published in all the papers about a year earlier. Mrs. Rogers' death had made the front pages which implied volumes about the family's social position.

The stunning woman was quite incongruous to the image he had built up in his mind of the type of woman he would meet at the vast cattle complex. Faded jeans and feeding a gray wolf pup from a bottle did nothing to blunt her elegance. The feelings he was having were so mixed up and confusing he could hardly concentrate on his driving.

Susan Rogers, sitting quietly beside the tall, silent wildlife specialist appeared to be totally occupied in the feeding of her young charges. One by one they were fed, and each time one had emptied its warm bottle, she would glance furtively at the rugged profile next to her. As she traded one pup for another from the washtub in the seat behind her, she would look at the man inquisitively. Something magnetic about Paul Taylor drew her interest. For the first time in a very long while, she was being attracted to a man. It was a disturbing feeling.

There had been many opportunities for romance for the young doctor even though she had grown up in virtual isolation in the remote recesses of the Montana rangeland.

Her premed days at the university had brought forth a plethora of young men anxious to vie for her attention. Some with honorable intentions and some with the obvious and single goal of getting her in bed. She was not only a beautiful and intelligent girl but she also had an arousing figure that could turn the head of the most discriminating young male.

However, there had been no nonsense in her objective of becoming a medical doctor and she had no time for social games. Finally, after she was admitted to medical school the rush for her favors had eased. No one had the time for it during that hectic period of learning.

She had been accepted at the exclusive Chicago Medical School, and after her academic and clinical training, she had taken her residency at Bellwood Memorial Hospital which had led to a position in the obstetrics department.

She could not have planned it better. At Bellwood she was able to reach a multitude of disadvantaged women grappling with unwanted, unexpected, and thoughtless pregnancies, guiding them through a comprehensive prenatal program and delivering healthy babies. It had been the most rewarding work she had ever done and had eclipsed her fondest dreams of helping the less fortunate in an unfair society.

It was there that it had happened. The young intern had sat down across from her in the hospital cafeteria at lunch one day about a year after she had joined the OB staff. He had introduced himself and politely asked if he could share her table since the hall was so crowded. Pleasant and apparently quite cultured, Susan found herself enjoying Raymond Wright's company every day at lunch.

She had never been away from home for such a long period of time, and the loneliness of life without friends in a big city swiftly caught up with her. Her dedication to the job left her with little time for anything else. Aside from her professional contacts, Susan had little social life. She had become starved for meaningful cultural exchange and dialogue. Her loneliness had begun to be a crushing burden, and the light-hearted but stimulating conversation she craved was satisfied daily by Wright.

In a few weeks their talks had become more serious, and he was finding the time to ask her to an occasional play or movie. She was well aware of the rigors of internship, and she was accommodating him whenever he could get free for a late dinner or show.

Ray had been dashing and attentive. An attractive man, he dressed nicely and maintained a well trimmed beard which tended to offset the premature balding he was experiencing. Although a little pudgy with the beginnings of a mild paunch around his middle, he was overall physically fit. Energetic and alert, he was stimulating company for the young obstetrician.

Under ordinary circumstances, Susan would have been more cautious. She should have recognized the age-old approach used by Wright. Maybe she didn't want to see it. She was at a vulnerable point in her life and willing to be a little careless for a chance to ease her loneliness — the most deprecating and debilitating word in the English language. It could reduce the human spirit to a level of despair that made even death seem attractive.

And it could certainly cloud sound judgment and good sense as Doctor Rogers was to find out.

****

One night Ray drove her to her apartment at a late hour, and she had invited him in because it had started to snow and the streets were getting slippery. The snow had not let up, and he had spent the night. The inevitable had happened.

Ray had been surprised to discover she was a virgin. Susan had tried to rationalize it all by telling herself she was almost thirty years old, and if she was ever going to get involved with a man, it had to be soon. Deep down, she knew she didn't love Ray Wright, but their relationship seemed to fill some indefinable void in her life. As if it were something a woman needed to do at some point in her life. An action that was expected of her in order to be considered normal and healthy.

Wright had moved in shortly after the memorable snow storm, and for six months they lived together. The way it ended would never be forgotten by Susan.

She had been sitting at her desk in the third floor OB wing when the phone had rung. It was Karen, the telephone switchboard operator.

"Dr. Rogers, I can't find Dr. Wright. He's not on his floor, and I have a telephone call for him that I think might be an emergency. Do you have any idea where I can reach him?"

Dear God, everybody must know of our affair, Susan thought as she listened.

"No, I don't, Karen, but I can try to track him down for you if you think it is an emergency," she offered.

"Would you mind talking to the lady, Doctor. She seems very distraught." Karen obviously wanted the matter out of her hands.

"Put her on, Karen," Susan replied. Ray's parents

lived in New Jersey, and immediately she thought it might be his mother.

"Thank you, Doctor Rogers. Pick up on line six." Then Karen was gone.

"Hello. This is Doctor Rogers," she had said hesitantly after pressing the six button.

"Doctor Rogers," a soft feminine voice had responded. "I'm Barbara Wright. I'm trying to locate my husband. It's an emergency. I've had to put our son, Jonathan, in the hospital." There had been a quality of distress in the woman's voice which she had tried to suppress.

Susan now had little recollection of what had transpired after that. She could remember taking the woman's number at the emergency room from where she was phoning and recalling her shaking hand when she replaced the receiver. She remembered madly searching the ward where Ray was supposed to be on duty and writing a note which she had placed on his desk.

Fifteen minutes later her phone had rung again. It had been the resident doctor who had been Ray's supervisor. Ray had been found coming in the rear of the hospital with a young nurse.

There had been no recriminations. No tears. Only one phone call. Ray Wright had packed his belongings and was out of her apartment and out of her life when she got home that night. He was also out of the hospital which was equally embarrassing for Susan.

The unexpected death of her mother about a month later heaped one anguish on another. Her father would never know the real reason for her decision to resign her position and return to the family ranch. He needed her now and would always view it as devotion and sacrifice on her part in giving up her career and coming back home. There was no way he could ever be told, although in retrospect she recognized it had been the only course of action she could have sensibly taken, the Wright affair notwithstanding. Her father could not have been left alone at his age with the responsibilities of the ranch on his shoulders. Selling the ranch was unthinkable, and it would have killed her father.

She should have known in the beginning that it would eventually come to that. That someday the ranch would be her responsibility. Going through the motions of becoming a doctor had been meaningless, and she hadn't looked far enough ahead to realize it.

On the other hand, someday the ranch would pass on to her entirely, and perhaps she could sell out and enjoy the career she had chosen and which had become so briefly fulfilling. No, that would never happen either. Rogers Ranch was too much of an institution to entertain that sacrilegious thought.

It looked like discontent would follow her regardless of her decision. There was only isolation and loneliness at the ranch. She had suffered it through all her growing years. Was she to lead a solitary existence her entire life? It didn't seem to matter which road she chose. Aloneness. She had seen its subtle evilness.

A girl in her dormitory at the university had squealed one day that she had finally been able to hug and kiss an old feral cat that she had been feeding for months. Heavens, wasn't there a member of the opposite sex of her own species the girl could have enticed to hug and kiss her? Especially with food?

Do we bring loneliness on ourselves? When she reflected on her own attempts to overcome that silent affliction, she saw she was hardly a notch above her dormitory sister. She had hugged and kissed a snake. All because of the most demeaning emotion a human being can have.

Looking at Paul Taylor, his eyes straight ahead on the narrow road, she reflected on the possibility of again having a relationship with a man. She had pushed the guilt of her affair with Raymond Wright into the recesses of her mind, and after a year it rarely assailed her thoughts. Yet, an affair with a married man, particularly one with children, would burden her forever. Her parents had been moral people, and she had grown up in a wholesome environment. Putting it all behind her and getting on with her life was easier said then done. Isolating herself on the ranch had helped in one respect but at the terrible price of giving up her professional life and chosen career.

She was drawn to Taylor's profile; the dark mane of hair neatly trimmed around the ears, the strong, chiseled jaw and chin, the attractive line of his nose. Susan was having difficulty keeping her eyes off him.

"Are you married, Taylor?" The words had slipped out and she immediately wished she could have retracted such an inappropriate question. Their relationship was strictly professional and she had just met the man.

"I used to be," he said easily, without taking his eyes from the road. "She died several years ago. In an automobile accident."

"I'm so sorry. I don't know what possessed me to ask such a personal question." But she did know. She had been thinking of Raymond Wright.

"Not at all. I understand you are a doctor." he said, turning his head and looking directly at her, his dark eyes alive and curious. She had opened the door for personal questions which was the direction in which he wanted their conversation to move.

"Yes, an obstetrician. But I don't practice anymore. After Mom died I decided to come home and take care of Dad. He needed help with the business." If only he knew the truth, she thought.

"I'll bet you are a good one. The way you handle animals is amazing." They were beginning to feel comfortable talking to each other.

Susan laughed. "At one point I wanted to be a veterinarian. I've always loved caring for animals. Dad talked me out of it."

"Considering all the cows and horses you have it seems to me it would have been a good decision."

"Yeah," she laughed again. "We have horrendous bills from Doc Ferguson's office every month. I could have saved us a bundle."

The young doctor's laughter had such a pleasant ring to it. Taylor had never been so captivated by a laugh before.

"Because of your profession I assume you are an animal lover also," she speculated.

"Well, most people that pursue wildlife management do so because of an interest in animals rather than a love for them." He caught himself too late. What a self-serving thing to say. He was about to get in a disagreement with this lovely lady.

"Of course," she answered back pleasantly. "I used the word in too broad a context. I meant it in terms of interest, compassion, caring. In the strictest sense I suppose love must be reserved for those to whom we grow close."

"Well put," he smiled. "We had an old dog once that

I loved. I didn't realize it until he died. It broke my heart that I never gave him the affection and attention I should have. Sometimes one can become very neglectful and not realize it until it is too late."

She turned her eyes to his. It was a poignant moment. Both understanding the other a little better.

"I expect he knew how you felt about him," she said softly.

"I hope so," he said.

He needed to change the subject.

"I should have talked to your father but didn't have the opportunity. So I'll have to tell you and discuss it with him later.

"For the record, I should point out to you that it's against the law to kill an endangered species animal except in certain cases of a predator destroying livestock. Even in those cases, and I presume your father's actions fall into that category, it's best to report the activity to us or Animal Damage Control or the Montana Department of Fish, Wildlife and Parks. We can then attempt to remove the animal and relocate it. There is always compensation for losses.

"There are very severe penalties for violating the Endangered Species Act, but since your dogs struck the wolf's trail at the site of a calf kill, we would hesitate to pursue such a case in court. However, if your father would kill or injure the dead wolf's mate without further provocation, we would be forced to act."

After going over the events of the hunt with Buck Dawson, he realized there would be great difficulty in a successful prosecution of this case. The strict and severe penalties for violating the Endangered Species Act were necessary in order to have meaningful enforcement of the

Act, and FWS could not afford to shirk its duty in applying the law.

On the other hand, the female wolf that was killed was clearly tracked from the dead calf to her den. It was prima facie evidence that could overwhelm a prosecution. In view of the controversial Wolf Recovery Program which had just started in Yellowstone, irreparable damage would be done to the project if FWS lost such a case in court. And perhaps even if they won.

There were further complications now to prosecuting wolf cases. It was an amendment to the Endangered Species Act declaring "experimental/nonessential" status to certain controversial species which included wolves. The amendment took away much of the full protection guaranteed wolves under the Endangered Species Act in areas where they did not occur naturally.

In addition, Colonel Roland R. Rogers would be a formidable adversary in court. His strong ties to state government including the governor, his connections with the Montana Stockgrowers Association, and his reputation in general would suggest that this was a case best left alone.

He didn't like lecturing this young woman and wanted to keep it as short as possible. After all, it was her father who had gone after the wolf, and she had no part in it, but his professional duty dictated that he make known to her the FWS policy. It was doubly difficult because she was doing strange things to his heart.

Susan wasn't going to defend her father's actions in the matter. The killing of the female wolf had upset her more than Paul Taylor would ever know.

"I'll talk to him when I get home. He calms down rather quickly. After a good nights sleep, he won't feel so collusive. Right now he's distraught because Red was his favorite dog."

Changing the subject abruptly, she continued, "You say you remove the animal and relocate it. How do you capture them?"

"We can sometimes trap them, but most times we tranquilize them. With bears it's necessary to move them great distances or they will come back. The criteria is to release them in good habitat. If they have plenty of food, they have less tendency to return to their original location.

"Most of our wolf problems stem from straying and overdepredation of the ungulate population in an area. Although the ranchers fear the wolves will destroy their livestock, it simply doesn't happen very often."

"Is that the reason for the opposition to putting wolves in Yellowstone?" she pressed. Being in the cattle business the polemic issue was well known to her.

Knowing Susan Rogers was a rancher of considerable clout, Taylor suspected she knew far more about the controversial wolf program than she was professing. Yet, she didn't seem to be taking sides.

"Partly," he answered. "Some of it comes from those that actually fear for their safety and the safety of their families. You can't laugh at that, but an attack on a human by a wolf is such a remote possibility the idea is ludicrous. Too many childhood stories of the big bad wolf, I guess.

"Actually," he continued, "we rarely have a wolf problem outside their known range, but if we do, as in your case, and we are fortunate enough to get the animal unharmed, it goes to the Yellowstone project. The ranchers should appreciate that. There's an ungulate abundance in Yellowstone, and we feel it highly unlikely there would be much long distance migration of wolves from there once they are established."

"You mean they wouldn't roam outside the park where they could get into sheep and cattle?" she asked.

"Our educated guess is there would be a very low incidence of it occurring. There has been and probably will continue to be an occasion instance of an individual separating from a pack and developing a chronic case of wanderlust," he laughed.

Taylor wasn't prepared for her next question. As always, he enjoyed talking about his work, particularly to those who showed an unprejudiced interest, but this lady was leading him.

"You're not convinced it was these pup's father that killed Big Red, are you?"

"I don't know," he answered honestly. "It's hard to believe. I've been in this business too long to make snap judgments. The idea that a wolf would come onto your premises and attack one of your dogs is a little hard to swallow. But then again, strange things can happen. I watched it snow on June 10 one year.

"When I relay this story to Wolfman he's not going to accept it without grave reservations. I'm certain of that. It sounds too . . . .too premeditated if that is the correct word. It would require an ability to reason which I don't think wolves have."

"I remember the time it snowed in June," Susan said. Then added, "I read recently about a scientific study to determine the intellect of certain animals. In this age of biological technology, don't we know this by now?"

"We know the brain capacity of most animals. That project you read about is to determine the range or spectrum of that capacity. In other words, we've always known some specimens are smarter than others of the same species. Do they get that way through rote? Age and experience? Or are there individuals who are simply smarter by virtue of exceptional brain power? As far as we now know, there is no indication of this in animals."

"But look how human intelligence has grown since Homo sapiens appeared on this planet. Why is it unreasonable to believe that animals have grown intellectually the same way? Genes play a big part in mental growth. When two superior individuals mate it usually results in superior offspring. Generationally, this has produced exceedingly smart individuals in humans over time. Why not in animals?"

It was clear the doctor thought she had a valid point.

Taylor pondered her words before answering.

"Wolves' greatest assets are their endurance and stamina followed closely by their intelligence. Their brain size is about thirty percent larger than dogs of comparable size. It may well be we have overlooked the mental capabilities of this species. But even if we have, it couldn't account for the alleged actions of this animal. He may be one smart wolf but to imagine he planned revenge on your dogs is quite a stretch." The biologist was without humor. "Frankly, I'm flabbergasted at the mere presence of the fellow. We keep tabs on all the Montana wolf packs, and I can almost assure you this wolf and his mate were not wanderers from any of them.

"I'm going to check with Wolfman when I get back to the office. If there have been any excursions of pairs from any of the packs we monitor, he will know about it."

"I wish Dad had left them alone. He's so unreasonable at times. I don't think wolves have attacked any of our livestock, and Buck Dawson doesn't think so either."

"I gathered as much when I talked to him," Taylor smiled.

"By the way," she said, wanting to get back to the happy prospect of raising the gray wolf puppy. "I've decided on a name for the little female."

"Look, don't get your hopes up. If Wolfman doesn't concur on this I can't go forward with it. I'm personally convinced you would do an excellent job of raising the pup. Probably better than the wolf gang in Helena, but I'm just one person in this equation." He knew it sounded like he was making excuses but he didn't want to see her grievously disappointed.

She acted like she hadn't heard him.

"I'm going to name her Gray Girl."

****

At Ferguson's Veterinarian Clinic, the venerable Dr. Wallace Ferguson met them with a broad smile. He knew them both.

"Hi Paul, Susan. Glad to see you." Nodding at the covered washtub they were carrying between them, he had a twinkle in his eyes. "I can't imagine what you have, but I'll bet it's going to be interesting."

The old vet had worked on more animals of Susan Rogers' than he cared to remember. His memory of her went back to when she was a little girl bringing in every kind of sick creature imaginable.

The wildlife biologist outlined what had happened with some occasional input from Susan.

"Doc," she said, "Taylor may be able to work out an

111

arrangement that would let me raise one of these pups. Could you give me a recommendation for the job?"

Ferguson had been probing and poking at the twisting, squirming things on a table while Susan held them. Watching her dexterity and fearless approach, Paul was impressed with her considerable talents in handling the wild animals. He suffered a stab of inadequacy watching her professionalism, and a feeling of warm admiration for the young woman came over him. He was glad Ferguson hadn't asked him to hold the slippery little demons while he examined them.

"Well, I would say you are eminently qualified to raise one of these babies," the old vet said. "In fact, you better leave your milk formula with us. It certainly is agreeing with them."

"I told her I couldn't promise anything. We had better leave them together here until I can look into it," Taylor spoke up. It was a practical suggestion, but Susan was reluctant to part with the small, white female. Nonetheless, she stayed silent.

"We'll go by the office. You can give Martha some necessary information, and I'll call Wolfman. It will all depend on him." Taylor hoped that would satisfy her.

****

Martha McKay was surprised to see the lovely young woman preceding Paul into the reception room. She wondered what was going on.

"Martha, this is Doctor Rogers. Martha McKay, our office manager," he said without further explanation.

Both women acknowledged the introduction politely.

"Martha, we're going to try to obtain an Endangered

Species Permit for Dr. Rogers so she can raise one of the baby wolves that were found. She can give you the required information while I call Helena." He had disappeared into his adjacent office before anything else could be said.

Martha had the intuition of a palm reader. Something told her Paul Taylor had just been knocked out of his socks by this beautiful blond Venus and was falling all over himself to accommodate her. As she asked the young doctor a few questions, she came to the realization of whom she was interviewing. Well, if it took a woman of this prominence to bring Paul back into the land of the living, it was fine with her.

Taylor had taken an inordinate amount of time on the phone. Susan remembered he had other things to talk to Wolfman White about besides her request, but she still was very uneasy. He probably was relating the entire wolf episode to White, and she speculated on what kind of spin he was putting on it. It would have to be favorable if she was to keep the baby wolf.

Finally emerging from his office, Taylor had a non-committal look on his face.

"Wolfman is going to prepare an affidavit. He said he could fax it down in about an hour."

"You mean . . . ," Susan stammered, still not sure what she was hearing.

"You get to keep the pup if final approval is made," he said, his face still showing nothing.

"Who gives final approval?" she asked, almost unable to breathe from anxiety.

"Well, it comes through the Department of Interior in Washington who will issue the formal permit, but my approval and the authorization from Wolfman should get the ball rolling," he said, with a hint of a grin.

113

"Oh, Taylor," she exclaimed. There was a look of pure joy on her face.

Martha had not missed the undisquised cuteness of her supervisor's remarks, and she was sure of it now. So unlike him. Something was going on here. Definitely.

"Don't get too excited." Taylor was frowning now over the girl's exuberance. "Gray Girl will have to be returned by next spring."

"I understand. Don't worry, I have no problem with that. She should be back with her own kind at the proper time, and I'm all for that." Susan's elation had not been dampened by the definitive time of return imposed on her.

"Now, why don't we have lunch. Wolfman's fax should be here when we get back, and you won't need to come back to town later. You can take the pup home with you today." It was now twelve o'clock, and he had a compelling urge to keep the exciting woman in his company as long as possible.

Susan frowned, "I hate to keep Pancho waiting. I've done that a few times, and he doesn't like it."

"No problem. I'll run you home later," Taylor persisted.

Martha, sitting there listening to this exchange, was astonished. The night before, Paul had indicated such anxiety to get back to the office early in order to wrap up the week's work. Now he was going to blow the whole afternoon taking this woman, whom he had just met, home.

"I can't let you do that, Taylor. Two trips to Rogers Ranch in one day is too much."

She sure wasn't protesting very strenuously, thought Martha.

Taylor was already thumbing through the telephone

directory for Simmons' Feed Store and then dialed the number.

"Yes," he spoke, "can you get a message to Pancho Rivera. He's there for some supplies for the Rogers ranch. He is? Fine. Tell him not to wait on Doctor Rogers. She will be returning to the ranch later. Tell Pancho to inform her father she should be home by four o'clock." He held the phone momentarily with his hand over the receiver. "OK?" he asked, a look of satisfaction on his face.

"OK," Susan answered. The plan suddenly sounded marvelous. She was going to get Gray Girl and take her home all in the same day.

****

Taylor had escorted her out of the office and to his Bronco in the parking lot. Martha's look had not been lost on him as they left. The Rogers woman's impact on him must be as obvious as if he had a sign around his neck proclaiming "I'm In Love".

Could Susan Rogers see it too? Was he being manipulated by her? Questions, questions. But, God, he felt good. He hadn't felt like this in years.

"Where are you taking me?" Dr. Rogers asked with mild concern. "I'm not dressed for any place fancy. I should have changed into more appropriate clothes before we left."

To Paul she looked like she would have complemented the Ritz even though she was wearing jeans. She wore casual clothes so tastefully she would have fit in at any restaurant in Billings.

"You like Italian?" he asked, ignoring her concerns.

"Sure," she grinned.

"Then you'll like this place. Don't worry, fancy it isn't. It's not far, we're almost there."

He had been making turns every block or two and seemed to be getting farther and farther away from the commercial section of the city. Susan had no idea where they were.

The Bronco turned onto a deserted street which had a line of buildings with very narrow fronts touching one another. Most of the buildings were empty, but near the middle of the row was one with a large ficus tree showing through the window. The single plate-glass pane next to the entrance had TONY GARA'S painted on it in large green letters. There was no parking lot but the street could easily park all the customers the small restaurant could hold.

"It's all right. You'll see," Paul told her reassuringly as they pulled in to the curb. The thought came to him that he may have made a horrible mistake. Maybe it wasn't all right. This lady was certainly not accustomed to dining in such ordinary culinary establishments.

Inside there were half a dozen tables and a row of stools along a narrow counter. Coming from the kitchen was a short, plump man of about fifty. He was dark with a bushy moustache. On his head was a chef's hat and a full apron hugged his round body. Obviously, he was proprietor, cook, and waiter combined.

"Paul," he greeted with gusto. "Glad to see you."

"Glad to see you too, Tony." Turning, he said, "Tony, this is Doctor Rogers. Doctor, this is Tony Gara, architect of Italian cuisine extraordinaire."

They all laughed as they shook hands.

Taylor knew Tony had shortened his name after coming to the United States. He was glad he had because

Taylor could never have pronounced his old country tongue-twisting name correctly. How Tony had ended up in Montana was anybody's guess and would remain an eternal mystery.

But there was no mystery as to why Gara was in the restaurant business. The man could cook the way Picasso had painted. He had made it an art form.

There were only two other customers in the place; two men seated at a far table. Paul had waved at the two after greeting Tony. Apparently, Gara had accumulated a group of Italian food lovers so loyal they had become acquainted with each other.

Paul and Susan selected a table near the kitchen entrance and Tony brought them menus.

"Tony's pasta salad with his own olive oil dressing is outstanding," Taylor commented, hoping he had not made a blunder by bringing her here.

"Sounds good to me." Susan folded her menu and looked around the small but immaculate eatery.

"Why is he so far off the beaten path? You could starve to death finding this place," she quipped.

Taylor leaned toward her in a confiding manner. "A few years ago Tony had the best Italian restaurant in the city. It burned one night along with his wife and daughter caught upstairs. He went through all the personal agonies of such a tragedy. Deep depression, alcoholism. Some of us – friends and customers –tried to help but nothing worked.

"He went into seclusion until last year when his support group rented this old building, bought some used restaurant equipment, a little paint and, presto, this is it. It was like a surprise party. One of the fellows enticed him out of his apartment and got him over here. Doctor, the man wept like a baby. Funny thing was, we all cried with him."

"And I suppose you were the ring leader," she said softly.

"Well, I was in on it. It was after I lost Carolyn and it was therapeutic for me. It is hard to explain. Knowing someone else's pain makes it easier to bear your own."

Tony was back and they both ordered the pasta salad and a glass of red wine.

Susan suddenly wanted to know more about this gentle man sitting across from her. She wanted him to continue talking.

"Is there more?" she asked, after Tony had left with their order.

"Not really, except it turned out so amazingly right. Tony has become interested in life again and has made this little hole-in-the-wall restaurant work. He has a dedicated following, and he can laugh and smile again. Just what we were all striving for." Tony's transformation apparently was a happy subject for Taylor, judging from the look on his face. "Best of all," he added with a chuckle, "he got back his zest for cooking, and we have all benefited from that."

Tony had come with their food.

"Doctor Rogers, I'm flattered you have visited my restaurant. I would also like to compliment you on your choice of escorts. Paul is one fine man."

"Hey, Tony, cut that out." Taylor was embarrassed by the patronizing words.

They ate in silence for awhile, and Paul watched with fascination as Susan's heaping salad disappeared. Maybe he hadn't made a mistake bringing her here after all.

"Taylor, that's the best pasta salad I've ever eaten in my life." She drained her wine glass and wiped her mouth daintily with the cloth napkin.

She had begun to see past the initial perception of common quality of Tony Gara's and was now noticing little things that reflected Tony's commitment to his small, neat business. The spotless table cloths, the cloth napkins, the sparkling silverware and crystal, the scrubbed floor, the cleanliness of the place, and the man himself — all had combined to deeply impress her.

"Do you think you could call me Paul? Just Taylor reminds me of an old college professor who used to bark at me," he asked in jest, although he had been mildly irritated at the condescending habit she had picked up. "He seemed habitually fond of saying, 'Taylor, this paper has no redeeming merit whatsoever'." They both laughed gleefully.

"If you will call me Susan, I'll consider it," she answered warmly.

****

Martha looked at the clock when the two returned after lunch. She was definitely sure now that something was brewing between them. An hour and a half lunch. Paul Taylor rarely took more than fifteen minutes.

The fax from Wolfman had arrived, and Paul read it over carefully. Then he let Susan read the authorization. It appeared satisfactory, so it was signed and copies made.

"An original and three copies will be forthcoming, Doctor. You will be receiving them in the mail along with an Endangered Species Permit from the Department of Interior in Washington. You should sign them, retain your copy, and send the rest back by return mail."

When they got in the Bronco again, this time to go to the clinic to pick up the female wolf pup, Susan turned to Paul and touched his arm.

"Taylor, I know you have put yourself out on a limb for me. You probably owe Mr. White big time. I just want you to know I'm aware of it, and I won't let you down. Gray Girl is going to get the best possible care." Her voice was low and intimate.

Paul felt his pulse quicken and his mouth had gotten dry. So dry he had trouble speaking.

"I only hope it doesn't break your heart when time comes to give her up," he responded.

****

The trip back to Rogers Ranch turned out to be a gabfest. Whereas the earlier ride into Billings that morning had been virtually in silence, now neither of them could get enough talking done. The obligatory remonstrations had been made and out of the way, and both of them now felt a compelling urge to chatter away.

Paul, who had always been the silent type, couldn't stop. With her prodding and rapt attention, he candidly told her his life history. Most of it was fresh in his mind, having dwelled on the days of his youth during the lonely drive out to the ranch that same morning.

He related the close association that had developed between him and Sam Howell. The outdoor experiences they had shared and Sam's sudden departure from this life. The profound influence the man had had on his growing up years and which had carried through to his professional life. How the green logbook Howell had given him had shaped him and he had become a wildlife statistician.

Then he told her about his family. How his father had

eked out a living on less than two hundred Wisconsin acres and a handful of Guernsey milk cows. The drive and determination of Charles and Virginia Taylor to see their three children through college. His older brother had become a lawyer, and his younger sister a school administrator. Almost storybook when the family history was reviewed in retrospect but far different in Paul's memory of the hardship and strife suffered by his parents.

"I envy you those close personal relationships. You had a rich growing up," Susan sighed. "I grew up virtually alone on the ranch. If I wanted a friend, I had to adopt an animal." There was no bitterness in her observations, only mild reflection and acceptance of her own early childhood circumstances.

Paul laughed, "I was always bringing home some sick or orphaned animal myself."

"We have a lot in common, don't we?" she stated somewhat intimately. Maybe it sounded too intimate, she decided so she added, "Animals, I mean."

Taylor had expected Doctor Susan Rogers to be distant and aloof. Instead, he found her to be warm, unassuming and down to earth.

Susan had expected Paul Taylor to be officious, busy being important, and afraid to expose any sensitivity. Instead, he was considerate, without veneer, and damn good-looking.

It was clear that they were mutually pleased to have met each other.

CHAPTER VII

Wolf had discovered a rise in the rolling grass about half a mile from the maze of buildings on Rogers Ranch. The grass was short enough to give him an unobstructed view of the ranch and close enough to see the two-legs as they moved about. Wolf's eyesight at a quarter mile could spot a prairie dog's head peering through wheatgrass, so he had no difficulty seeing the detailed ranch activity from his surveillance point. The thick grass gave him plenty of cover if he lay on his belly.

He had started his vigil early. Coming down off the high mountain at dawn after a short sleep, he had stopped to drink at a stream being drawn from the high country toward the Musselshell River basin. Bubbling and gushing as it exited the high terrain, the water became quiet but swift when it got to the two-legs' land. The spring thaws now had the water rushing although normally the stream would be lazy and placid as it flowed through the grassland. It wandered close to the knoll Wolf had found and would prove to be convenient.

Paralleling close to the edge of the water, a muskrat provided him with the only food he had been able to find for three days. The events of the night before were welded in his mind, and the adrenaline was still pulsing through his veins as he ate. Watching from the knoll, a plan of action began to form in his mind.

They would come; he was sure of that. But he hadn't expected the additional dogs that came in to the ranch about mid-morning in the back of a rolling object. There were three of them. The two remaining dogs that lived at the ranch would make five. He didn't like it, but there was little he could do.

Prior to the arrival of the rolling thing full of dogs, another two-legs' carrier had arrived, but it had left soon after. It had come with one and then left with two two-legs.

Wolf's mind was racing. The barking dogs were eager, knowing they were going to hunt so there would be little delay. In all probability, the dogs and hunters would go directly to the high mountain where they would expect to find Wolf near the den. He knew exactly what their routing would be. If he crossed the north pasture and headed for the ill-fated lair, chances would be good that the dogs would pick up his trail quickly. That's what he wanted to happen. He would deviate to the east when he heard the dogs strike his scent and head for the dead-end ravine. It was there Wolf would lead the dogs.

He had hunted in the box canyon many times, but it had taken several cautious ventures in before he had learned it was possible to get out of it without retracing his steps. The passage abruptly ended against a shear, stone cliff rising at the end of the deceitful gorge. Near the end was a ledge he could jump to, and from there another leap would put him on ground where he could scramble to the top.

Only with practice had he learned exactly how to do it. It had always been a good place to hunt because unwary animals could not escape once they were trapped in the one-way draw. Knowing he could exit without back-tracking made hunting the canyon safe and was one of his favorite places to trap quarry.

He was planning it carefully, but the additional dogs complicated the scheme. Thinking about the new dogs, he didn't like the odds, but his hatred for the two-legs' dogs kept his resolve at a fever pitch. There would be five of them. Wolf despised them all, but he would concentrate his vengeance on only the two dogs that had played a part in destroying his family.

There would be no problem identifying them. Their straining, yowling faces would torment his memory forever. His revenge would change their gleeful baying to whimpering terror, and their loud bravado would be exposed for what it really was — a cover-up for the weakness and fear all dogs developed from association with the two-legs.

There was ancestral wolf in every dog, but being wild and free separated the two like the night and the day. Somewhere in the separation the dog had become weak and dependent on the two-legs, willing to do their bidding and turning on their own kind. In the process, they had become vile and contemptible to all the free spirits of the world.

Wolf had no familial bond with any of them nor any compassion for their existence.

****

It was a few minutes before four o'clock when Paul

and Susan drove through the entrance to Rogers Ranch. The timing had been perfect, and Colonel Rogers wouldn't be worried about his daughter. What he would say when he saw she had returned with one of the wild wolves was another matter. Paul sensed, however, the power Susan possessed over her father. The old man ruled everyone with a loud, exigent voice except her. With Susan his tone would soften, and she would turn him into warm clay, soft and malleable. Ready to acquiesce to her every desire. Taylor admitted to himself she had the same effect on him.

"Something's going on, Taylor," she exclaimed, sitting upright in the Bronco as they drove up to the parking area in front of the house.

A pickup was pulling out from the barn lot with three dogs tied in the back, barking and straining against their leashes. The truck was leaving, and as it passed the Bronco, Susan recognized their neighbor, Bill Colby, driving and another man she didn't know sitting in the passenger seat. It appeared Colby deliberately avoided looking at her when the truck passed, though they were good friends. Colby's farm was about twenty miles to the south.

Looking toward the barn, Susan saw a cluster of men gathered around something lying on the ground.

"Dear God," she breathed, jumping from the Bronco at a dead run.

Pancho saw her coming and ran to intercept her.

"No, Missy. No, Missy," he wailed. "The lobo killed Max and Beethoven," the distraught Mexican shouted. He didn't want her to see the dark forms lying in the dirt near the barn and tried to block her path.

Buck Dawson saw her coming too and had detached himself from the circle of men.

"What happened, Buck?" she asked urgently.

"Like Pancho said, the lobo killed the dogs," he stated in his slow drawl. He looked accusingly at Taylor who had followed close behind Susan.

"Yes, but how, dammit?" she demanded.

"I wasn't there, Miss Susan. Maybe Cody can tell you better than me. All I know is the colonel called old man Colby this morning after you left to bring his dogs over here, and they struck out after the lobo. When they got back, our two dogs were dead." Buck turned and hooted for Watkins.

The young cowboy approached slowly, nervously gripping his wide-brimmed hat with both hands, the mane of red curls unruly outside the confines of the hat. His eyes showed fear of a reprimand from his female boss. He had never felt very comfortable in her presence despite the fact that the crush he had for her had escalated to rapturous love after she had mounted the unbroken and high-stepping bay horse bareback in the barn lot and rode the prancing devil clean out of sight. It had happened a few years earlier, but Watkins had never forgotten it. It may have been more admiration than love, but whatever it was, he had never gotten over it, and the diminutive cowboy had become her slave forever.

"Tell Miss Susan what happened, Cody," Buck spoke up.

"I ain't real sure myself, Ma'm." Watkins sensed they had had no business out there chasing the gray wolf. It had been a stupid thing going after the lobo. They had already killed his mate and taken his young, but he had only responded to orders from the colonel. "He must'a been real close to the ranch 'cause we picked up his trail soons we let the dogs loose. Took them dogs for a merry chase, I'll tell you. Clean on the other side of Bear Mountain and up a blind gulch. Them dogs got so far ahead of us, they weren't no way we could get there in time.

"But, lord-god, we could hear the beller'n and the howl'n. We knew something was gett'n its killing done. When we finally did make it in there, we found Max dead and old Beethoven so bad we had to put him out'n his misery. And there weren't no wolf or nothing else."

"You mean no one saw what the dogs were chasing?" Susan asked with surprise.

"No Ma'm. And he could'na run out of there. We'da seen him and the other dogs would'a been right behind him. They was just jumping around and barking at nothing but the bare canyon walls." Watkins had gotten excited in the telling of the bewildering tale and was trying to make a big mystery of it, which in truth it seemed to be.

"Where's Dad?" she asked, directing her eyes toward Buck. It was all her fault, she admonished herself. Her father had told her he was going to get the wolf. Why had she gone off merrily to town knowing the state of mind he was in?

"He's in the house, Miss Susan. The colonel is all right but you might want to stay out of his way for awhile."

Turning to Taylor who had been standing close by and listening intently, she said, "Come on, Taylor. You too, Pancho."

The hunters had scattered, all in a roundabout way wanting to get to the sanctuary of the bunkhouse and a safe distance from the colonel's daughter. They had suffered the tongue of the colonel, and they weren't anxious for a lecture from the young doctor too.

Pecky Woodall, String Starcher, and Ed Hastings stood outside the building until all the hands who had taken part in the hunt had gathered, ostensibly to hold their own little discussion of the ill-fated hunt. Pecky started the diatribe, a favorite ploy of his to get something brewing. "Well, Cody, looks like old Billy was right. That lobo's still invisible." Billy Greateyes, sitting against the bunk- house on his three-legged stool looked on inexpressively.

The colonel had started the popular practice of call- ing the gray wolf a lobo. It was a misnomer since a lobo was a Mexican wolf; however, the ranch men had picked up on the name because it sounded menacing and demonic. Watkins knew Pecky was wanting to have some fun at his expense, but he was in no mood for it.

"Listen, man. You give me some good dogs, and I'll go after a half starved grizzly. But, man. . . .that thing . . . . he went after the dogs. And Max and Beethoven was good dogs. So was Big Red. The colonel brings in anymore dogs with the idea of catching that thing, he can count me out. I ain't having no part of it." A rueful finality was unmistakable in Watkin's voice, and the last vestige of Pecky's humor dissipated among the somber crowd. What had happened was no joking matter, and Watkin's rare seriousness had infected them all with a contagious sense of foreboding and anxiety. Watkin's mood had even rubbed off on Pecky, who for once was at a loss for words. He could only stand by with a fading grin and bobbing Adam's apple.

At that moment Roland Rogers couldn't have orga- nized a clay pigeon shoot among his men.

****

Susan, Paul, and Pancho had walked back to the Bronco and had wrestled the large washtub out of the back seat.

"Pancho, you take this pup to the barn. Put her in the first empty stall and stay there with her until I get back. You understand?"

"Si, Missy, si, si." It didn't take much to frighten the timid old handyman, and his eyes were rolling with apprehension. The killing of Max and Beethoven had just about done him in.

They found the colonel in his study, a partly filled liter of Scotch on his desk.

"Where the hell have you been?" he growled, not even looking up at the two standing in the doorway.

"Didn't Pancho give you the message?" Susan asked, a little perplexed.

"He didn't say you were going to be running around all day with this . . . . . this moon-eyed wolf lover." The colonel slammed down his empty glass loudly on the desk, looking up at them with blood-shot eyes.

"Dad!" screamed his daughter.

"It's all right, Susan. He's upset. I'll let myself out," Taylor whispered and then was gone.

****

Tony was closing up when he heard the pecking on the glass front door. When he saw who it was, he hurried to the door and let Paul in. Taylor sure didn't look like the man who had eaten lunch there that same day with the exquisite blond lady.

"You OK? You look like hell. What happened?" Tony was baffled.

"I'm all right. You got anything to drink?" Taylor asked.

"Sure. Come on back." The squat proprietor locked the door and turned out the front lights before leading the way to the back room kitchen.

Solemnly, Tony retrieved a bottle of bourbon and a glass. Something told him Taylor wasn't much interested in his best vino. Tony never drank now that he was a recovering alcoholic. Keeping a bottle of spirits in plain view kept him honest.

It wasn't until Taylor had poured himself a second drink that he spoke. Tony sat silently across from him at the round kitchen table watching the haggard man.

"I should have known it wouldn't work. What in the hell happened to me? I'm not even in those people's world. I provide a service for those kind and that's all. Ordinary people can't even be friends with such elitists, let alone anything else."

"What you talking about, man?" Tony wanted to know.

"How could I have ever imagined such a thing happening?" Taylor continued, talking mostly to himself and ignoring the question. He was really feeling sorry for himself as the second slug of straight liquor hit his stomach. It also loosened his tongue, and finally the full story was related to the sympathetic Italian.

"It was her old man, Paul, not her. Sounds to me like she's quite a woman. From what I saw of her today, you would be a fool to walk away from this. Give her a chance, and give yourself a chance too.

"This is what you have needed since Carolyn died. Someone to snap you out of it like you guys did for me." Tony was talking to him like a Dutch uncle.

Taylor wasn't listening. "It can't work, Tony. She's

rich, high society, impeccable breeding, smarter than I am. Hell, she's a doctor. What can I do? Muck around with animals. Take surveys, count the birds, juggle statistics. Bull shit!" He was slowly getting drunk. It was something he hadn't done since his college days.

"Come on, Paul. This woman has struck a cord with you. You wouldn't be this upset if she hadn't. I don't think you're being fair to her. Or to yourself. You're too damn sensitive. Her old man just lost all his dogs, for God's sake. I wouldn't have gotten around him if he was the pope."

"Tony, can I spend the night? I can't stand the thought of being alone in that damn apartment tonight."

"Of course. I got a day bed in the hall. You got no business driving anyway. Besides, I got to get some food in you."

"To hell with food. I want to get drunk."

"You're well on your way, man. Well on your way."

They sat up talking most of the night. Until the alcohol put Taylor in a stupor and Tony had to lead him to bed.

****

Paul always spent Saturday mornings at the office. It was the only time he could get any meaningful work done. No one else came in on Saturdays so he could concentrate and plan for the coming week. He had killed the entire day on Friday dealing with the wolves and had gotten disturbingly behind on the week's work.

The wildlife conference in Helena was scheduled for the following week, and he wanted to prepare for that too. Wolfman White would be there, and it would be an opportunity to talk to him about what had transpired at the Rogers ranch. There had to be some logical explanation for what had happened that had escaped him. Wolves were incapable of conscious revenge. They killed to satisfy hunger. Pure and simple. Aberrant behavior might be possible, but experience discounted that theory.

He didn't reach the office until ten o'clock. Glad to see no one else was there to see his obvious hangover, at least he had felt well enough to run by the apartment to shower, shave, and change clothes.

After Carolyn's death he had sold their suburban home and applied the equity on a duplex in town. It had worked out well since he had managed to rent one-half to a young working couple. He occupied the other side. The young people were quiet and congenial, no children, and the rent almost made the payments on his mortgage. He was seldom home, and the couple had been happy there with the added privacy.

The light was bright on the answering machine when he came in the office, and he debated whether or not to listen to the call. He had a lot to do. Curiosity overcame his resolve, however, and finally he punched the playback button.

"This is Susan Rogers. I'm trying to reach Paul Taylor. Please leave a message for him to call me. He has my number. Thank you."

The machine clicked off.

There was a scowl on his face, but his pulse was pounding. Why did her voice do that to him? he marveled with some irritation.

The light came back on and clicked off again. No message. Three more times it happened, and Taylor was sure it had been Susan repeatedly calling. Some perverse feeling made him smile sardonically. "To hell with her", he exclaimed to an empty office.

In fifteen minutes the phone rang.

"Fish and Wildlife," he answered as professionally as he could. He knew it was going to be her.

"Taylor! Where have you been? You didn't go home last night." Susan's tone was not accusing but sounded more like sudden relief that she had finally reached him.

For some reason it made him defensive. What business was it of hers where he had been? And where had she gotten his home number? Then it occurred to him that a Billings directory was probably at the ranch, and he was listed.

"So?" he answered testily.

She ignored his tone of voice. "Taylor, I want to apologize for Dad, and he wants to apologize too. His behavior yesterday was inexcusable. He feels terrible about it." Her voice was soft and sincere. It had that irresistible quality that melted his heart and made him feel like a lemming being lured to the sea.

As she talked he could feel his resentment dissolving. "OK, apology accepted but not really necessary. I understand he was just lashing out at whomever got in his way after losing his dogs so brutally."

"No, it was indefensible regardless of what happened." Both knew it had been the Scotch talking.

"Well, it's over and forgotten as far as I'm concerned." Harboring ill-will had never been a part of Paul's make-up. Moreover, her voice had wrung all the anger from his system.

"Thanks, Taylor." There was a long pause. "Rozi is off on Sundays, and I always cook Sunday dinner. Tomorrow

I'm planning on fried chicken. I know it's short notice but could you come?"

"I'd like to, Susan, but I have to go to Helena tomorrow for a three day wildlife conference. It starts Monday morning, so I plan to drive over Sunday afternoon." It was not just an excuse. He found himself desperately wanting to see Susan Rogers, and all the resentment that had boiled over within him the previous evening had turned into a simmering craving.

"Will you be seeing Wolfman White?" she asked.

"Yeah."

"Thank him for me."

"Sure."

"Are you going to talk to him about the wolf?"

"He's going to think I'm crazy," Taylor laughed. "Can you imagine him believing a wolf killed your three dogs?"

"Will you be back Friday?"

"Actually, Thursday," he said.

"Could we have lunch again? My treat this time."

Paul's heart leaped, and a wave of excitement swept over him.

"I'd like that," he said, desperately trying to keep his voice even.

"I'll call you Friday morning about where we can meet."

"OK."

"See you then," she said as she rang off.

Taylor sat holding the phone for several minutes. The woman could mold him like the Franklin Mint, and there was nothing he could do about it. She had gone out of her way to arrange another meeting between them. Why would she do that if she didn't like him? Maybe he was wrong about these people. Was her conscience bothering her? Did she feel an obligation to him for his help in getting to keep Gray Girl? Or could she possibly be feeling about him the way he was feeling about her?

That possibility was so remote it defied contemplation.

****

It was a long week. Wolfman had indeed thought him crazy when told about the gray wolf killing all the Rogers dogs. Being a wolf specialist, his experience with the species prevented him from accepting any part of the far-fetched tale. He quickly picked up on the fact that no one had seen the predator which ended it as far as he was concerned.

"Paul, I've known you a long time. I must be slipping not to have noticed you going off the deep end. Everybody says you been going at it too hard. You ever thought about that possibility?"

"Everybody goes at it too hard, Cas. That's what's wrong with the world.

"Look, all I'm doing is telling you what has happened over at Rogers Ranch. You're the wolf specialist. It's your job to sort these things out, not mine."

"Don't put that gorilla on my back, old friend. I don't have any answers for wolf stories like that, and I've been in the business of wolves for twenty-five years."

"OK, Cas, OK. All I want is a little help. A little help." Taylor also had no answers. If Wolfman White couldn't shed light on the Rogers wolf mystery, then who could?

Wolfman hadn't been too happy about being talked into issuing the authorization to let the Rogers woman keep the wolf pup either. But he respected Paul Taylor's judgment in the matter. Their professional relationship spanned many years, and White regarded Taylor as one of the best in his field.

During the first evening of the three day conference, a group of the wildlife professionals was having dinner together in downtown Helena. Taylor arranged to sit next to Casper "Wolfman" White.

"Cas, I'm still trying to sort through the mystery of that wolf story at the Rogers Ranch. I know what you think but mind if I ask you a few more questions?" Paul had already pestered the wolf specialist enough, but he wasn't satisfied. He couldn't let it die.

"Don't know what more I can add, Paul, but go ahead, shoot." Wolfman, a middle-aged, plumpish man sported a shaggy beard with enough salt and pepper in it to actually resemble a wolf's coat. His straight, long nose ending over small, thin lips gave him a definite wolfish look. Maybe it was because everyone was thinking wolf when they addressed White, but most people actually thought he had acquired the nickname because of the resemblance rather than an off-shoot of his professional specialty.

"I think we should start with the basics such as where those wolves came from, if indeed there was a male with that female." Taylor had never questioned the presence of another wolf. The howling from the mountain had been real enough in his judgment. Only the acts of killing the Rogers dogs were questionable. No one had seen the elusive animal. "What about the packs up in Glacier and those scattered down toward the Bitterroots?" he continued.

"Paul, there are probably less than seventy wolves throughout Glacier National Park. We keep tabs on those so closely we know where they will be moving every day before they know themselves. The wolves between the Bitterroots and the Divide are checked the same way. It's necessary because of the public perception of the animals as highly predatory to livestock.

"We get an occasional pair down out of British Columbia or Alberta, but they most always stay west of the Divide. No way they would leave the mountains and migrate all the way over to the Rogers ranch. It's too far south and much too far east.

"As far as the new packs in Yellowstone are concerned, admittedly they have not stabilized to the point where they are predictable. But at the same time we are monitoring their movements and numbers with intense scrutiny for reasons you are well aware of. The Idaho releases have spread out in several directions, but none have been moving very far eastward.

"Again, a footloose pair in Yellowstone or central Idaho would not opt for the wide open range north of Billings. They would be drawn like a magnet to the security of the remotest mountain terrain they could find.

"Which ain't Rogers Ranch," he added with finality.

Wolfman's words were always gospel. Taylor could not dispute the man's assessment.

"Then where in the devil did those wolves come from? Aren't you a little curious about this entire matter? Even if you don't believe a wolf killed the Rogers dogs, you should at least be a little inquisitive about where they came from," Taylor suggested.

"Curious and inquisitive, yes. Answers, no." Wolfman responded with a shrug of mock despair.

"What about Saskatchewan?" Taylor asked.

"No packs near Montana. They are all very far to the north, best as I recall," White answered. He seemed to be engrossed in thought for several seconds. "Tell you what. I know Dominick LeBare up in Regina pretty well. He's my Canadian counterpart in Saskatchewan. If you want, I'll give him a call. Last time I spoke with him he mentioned a pack up there that had been roaming well south of their previously known range. I remember he had some concerns about it."

"Thanks, Cas. I'd really appreciate that. Mysteries like this really bug me. I sure would like to get to the bottom of this." Taylor felt he had stumbled onto a lead. It was the only one he had. "Plus, I'd like to reestablish my credibility with you," he laughed.

"You sure you're not involved with this doctor woman you been putting everyone out for?" Wolfman asked jokingly.

Taylor grinned sheepishly but said nothing. Vigorous protest tells a multitude of secrets, he thought. Besides, there was certainly no involvement, as Wolfman had put it, nor would there likely be any.

Not that he didn't want it to happen but the obstacles were simply too daunting. He had never considered himself a dreamer. Maybe he was and didn't know it. When he had an occasional realistic thought, he could see how hopeless it all was.

The three days in Helena had given him some time to assess his sudden attraction to the stunning Rogers woman. The quantum leap from no interest at all in women to head-over-heels in love with one, all in the time frame of a deep sigh, was so foreign to his nature that he had difficulty accepting it. From a logical and practical standpoint, the romance didn't have a chance. There was no common ground because of the wide social and cultural differences that

separated them. The grandeur of the woman was overpowering. Her effortless grace and charm shining through even
while being nursemaid to wild wolves. Her inalienable
beauty and elegance despite the ruffled hair, faded jeans
and scuffed riding boots.

Intellectually, he would never grow to her level. What
made it all so frustrating was knowing circumstances prevented him from ever achieving her benchmark in life.

But love did funny things to the heart. It could subdue
the most obvious obstacles and make them seem frivolous
and unimportant. He couldn't discount the fact it was she
who seemed anxious to keep their relationship going. She
had her wolf and could have kissed him off with no further
contact at all. At least until next spring when she would be
required to give up the young animal.

No, her nature was more gentle than that, he reflected. If she really wanted to end their budding relationship,
she would be subtle and kind enough to ease him out of her
life gently. Maybe that was what she was going to do.

Then again, he wasn't a bad-looking guy. Lots of
girls had been attracted to him. She could do a lot worse.
Perhaps she felt the same attraction he felt. It was possible.

No, he was no Romeo. No ladies' man. She could
easily find bigger fish than him.

As these crazy, silly thoughts coursed through his
mind, he laughed to himself. He was thirty-five years old and
thinking like a sixteen year old.

The week dragged on slowly, mostly because of
Paul's anxiety to see Susan again. Irrespective of his
conviction that there was no future for their relationship, he
fervently hoped it would continue. He kept thinking of their
date to have lunch on Friday. Was she going to take him to

some high-class restaurant in town to impress him since she had insisted on paying? Perhaps she was doing it to even up her social obligation for the impromptu lunch the week before.

Assenting to this headstrong woman and not ending it when he had the chance was going to create far more pain in the long run, he suspected. But he had been completely helpless against her soft, persuasive voice, and deep inside he knew when he did see her again and those searching blue eyes locked his, he would be forever lost. All his reservations would vanish as quickly as a spring rain.

****

Susan had a lousy week also. The colonel's continuing bad mood was becoming a burden for her and everyone at the ranch. The cowboys were avoiding him, particularly the hunting party that had witnessed the results of the terrible altercation on Bear Mountain. Even Buck tried to keep things running with as little contact as possible with his employer.

Dawson had begun to notice that Miss Susan was issuing most of the orders pertaining to ranch management lately and that suited him just fine.

Susan was still castigating herself for not recognizing the lengths and extent of her father's behavior, so wrongly or rightly, she shared the blame for the deaths of Max and Beethoven. Their loss had broken her heart, and she was angry, first at her father and then at herself during the entire week.

The tall biologist was constantly on her mind. Could she be falling in love with Paul Taylor? Please, no. She had suffered enough from her affair with Raymond Wright. She had fancied herself in love with him too at first and look what had happened. It had been the lowest point in her life, and for her own sake she couldn't take the chance of having another relationship with a man that didn't love her.

Taylor couldn't have much sincere feeling for her if he could walk away over a silly, thin-skinned hurt from her father. Had she not called to apologize, probably she would never have heard from him again. Maybe a letter, very official, informing her of her obligations under the terms of the authorization to keep the wolf. The thought made her laugh derisively.

The only solace she found during the long week was Gray Girl. The pup was tolerating her now and already showing signs of growing, or so it seemed to Susan. She had begun taking the young animal outside in the backyard to play in an attempt to gain the wolf's confidence and was happy with the progress she was making.

The colonel had forbidden her to horseback ride into the mountains which had confined her riding to the range-land. Riding around among the cattle was boring. Even Little Joe didn't like it. The spirited gelding loved charging up the mountain trails and galloping along the high ridges. On the range only a slow jog was allowed because the tall grass concealed so many holes. Plus, there were no spectacular views to be found in the flat sameness. On the Bear the beauty of life could be seen in all its splendor, and the magnitude of the world could stir the soul.

Susan loved the high mountain trails because of those magnificent vistas. She could see the rolling grass stretching for miles in a wave of green and bronze when they were high on the craggy ridges. She loved to view it from there but hated riding in it on the range floor. There was an overlook with a large boulder to sit on and eat a picnic lunch while gazing fifty miles. Maybe it was a hundred miles. She didn't really know. She had named the spot Susan's Retreat. Surrounded by scrubby white-barked pines, it gave her a feeling of private contentment unlike anything she had ever experienced.

Living in the remote region of central Montana should have afforded her all the solitude she wanted, but sometimes she sought even more. It was her secret place. It was her last best place.

She had ridden only a couple of times all week because of her father's restriction and this added to her depression. Whiling away the hours with Gray Girl helped, and they romped every day in the green grass of the back-yard. She thought Friday would never come, but finally the day arrived. Then she waited impatiently for eight o'clock which was the earliest she felt she could call Taylor's office. She had been up since five. Pancho would leave for Billings around nine.

Surprisingly, Taylor answered the phone himself.

"Good morning," she said cheerfully.

"Well, good morning to you too," he laughed. Her voice awoke that familiar warm feeling that came over him every time he talked with her.

"Sorry to be calling so early. I was afraid I might not get you before Pancho leaves for town," she explained.

"You could have called earlier. I was in by seven."

"Really? Are you a workaholic?"

"I don't think so. I just never seem to get caught up," he chuckled.

"No wonder. Having to put up with people like me

with their silly demands on your time."

"You talking about lunch, or what?"

They both laughed. Being comfortable with one another again made the laughing come easily.

"Yes. Are we still on for today?" she asked.

"As far as I'm concerned we are," he replied. "Where can I meet you?" He couldn't tell her he had thought of nothing else all week.

"How about Doc Ferguson's? Pancho knows how to get there and we can check on the other pups."

"Hey, that sounds like a good idea. How's Gray Girl doing?"

"Growing like a weed and mean as a half-starved sidewinder. I think she is wanting to be weaned. She's destroying everything in her reach. From pencils to table legs," Susan said with resignation. "A dog, she isn't."

"Get her a bone."

"Way ahead of you. The kitchen is beginning to look−and smell−like a wolf den."

"It's going to get worse as she grows. What are you going to do?"

"I'll keep her in the kitchen as long as I can. Pancho has cleaned out one corner for her where the destruction will be limited to stone and iron," she laughed. "Dad's taking it all far better than I expected."

"You asked for it. And, I might add, got no encour-agement from me." Taylor was laughing too. Then his tone changed. "Be careful. If she should bite you, we would have a problem. A big problem. Rabies, you know."

"Don't worry, Expert," she teased.

"Well, finally a name other than Taylor. Are we moving toward more familiar ground?"

"I don't like the way you say familiar."

They both laughed again.

"If Pancho doesn't want to take you to Doc's, I can pick you up at the feed store." The store where Pancho purchased their weekly supplies was well known to Taylor. He hoped she couldn't detect the urgency in his voice. He could hardly wait to see her again.

"No, Panch won't mind running me out to Doc's clinic but I doubt either of us could find Tony Gara's."

Paul was more than mildly surprised. "You want to have lunch at Tony's?"

"Of course. Once you find these treasures you stick with them. Just like Montana," she quipped. Montana was known as the Treasure State. "See you at Doc's about twelvish. I think Panch is getting ready now to leave. I don't know how Rozi puts up with that man. No patience whatsoever." She rang off with a fading laugh. It was the same giggle that Paul had found so appealing and fascinating.

The short conversation had sent him soaring like mercury in a hot room, and he dreaded seeing Martha McKay when she came in at eight-thirty. She would know in an instant that he had been talking to the Rogers woman.

****

Susan was convinced Taylor had called ahead. Tony was really prepared for them. He had rattled off a host of dishes that weren't on the luncheon menu and waited patiently for their decision.

Ordering a small green garden salad with Tony's special dressing and a small dish of Fettucine Alfredo with chicken bites, Susan stressed small in no uncertain terms.

Paul selected a chilled pasta primavera and wished he had also told Tony to make it small. When it came, small it wasn't. Tony's own red vino made the meal smooth and delectable.

The rotund Italian feigned distress that they had ordered so skimpily, but they saw he was secretly pleased with their reaction to his food. Both Susan and Paul suspected he had gone all out for them and wished they could have eaten more. The meal had not been elaborate but delicious, and when it was over they had that satisfying feeling that only good food can bring to the body.

At the conclusion of the meal, Taylor excused himself saying he should check in at the office. Being gone for an hour at lunch was foreign to him, and he felt compelled to call Martha.

While he was talking on the phone in the kitchen, Tony approached their table.

"May I?" he asked.

"Certainly. Sit down," Susan smiled.

"Doctor Rogers, I must say to you that Paul Taylor is a very fine man. I've known him for many years. He saved me from self-destruction. I hope you don't think I'm meddling but I wanted . . . . . ." He was at a loss for words and became hopelessly unable to express his thoughts.

"Thank you, Tony. You are not meddling at all. I really appreciate your candor. I'm glad you are his friend. He's got a good one." She was so touched by the sincerity of the round-eyed man that a tear clouded her vision.

Tony wanted desperately to make the doctor aware of Taylor's hopes and fears without offending either one of them.

"He spent the night here last Friday. He was very

145

unhappy. I think he likes you maybe more than you know."
Tony was having difficulty again. It really wasn't any of his
business but Paul was a friend and benefactor. Tony was
also a romantic and thrived on seeing people happy. It may
have been an offshoot or rebound from his own unhappy
years.

They saw Taylor returning and Tony jumped up nervously.

"The meal was delicious, Tony," Susan said, also
rising. "But please, cut back a little next time. If I ate here
all the time, I wouldn't be able to get into anything I own.

"Don't worry, Doctor, I serve only guilt-free dishes to
beautiful people like you and Paul. So you stay beautiful. I
only indulge old fat men like myself." His eyes were twinkling
and his laughter infectious.

They had had a good time.

Paul drove her to Simmons Feed Store where they
spotted Pancho sitting in the loaded pickup.

"He's a dear," Susan smiled. "A pill sometimes but
a dear man the rest of the time."

"It's obvious he is near the top of your very extensive
and thriving fan club," Paul said.

She looked at him through blue eyes expressing true
feelings. "I enjoyed lunch. Not only the excellent food but
the very nice company." He had insisted on paying.

"Thanks," he muttered, feeling like a love-struck kid.
She had to see it. In his eyes, in his voice, and in the flush
of his face, but there was absolutely nothing he could do to
control his emotions.

Paul escorted her to the truck and opened the door.
Turning, she said, "How about dinner Sunday? It'll be fried
chicken again. It's Dad's favorite so I cook it a lot."

"I love fried chicken. What time?" he responded heartily. He had regained his composure.

"Come early. We can take a ride. You do ride, don't you?" She was smiling, a teasing twinkle in her eyes.

"It's been awhile, but I can manage if you don't give me some outlaw horse," he laughed.

"Dad won't let me ride up on the mountain since he thinks the wolf might still be around. It should be all right if you are with me. I'll show you a secret place," she confided, although Pancho was listening to every word they uttered.

Pancho rolled his eyes and started the engine. Colonel Rogers ain't gonna like this either, he decided to himself.

CHAPTER VIII

Paul arrived early. Maybe too early but he had been restless and couldn't wait to get started. He was possessed with an inner need to be in the presence of the taffy-haired, blue-eyed doctor. This time there was no reminiscing on the lonely, long drive north. There was only anticipation and a constant image of the beautiful woman with stars in her eyes who had inextricably stirred his senses.

He was concerned about his relationship with the colonel and prepared himself mentally for the rancher's hostility. Under the adverse circumstances of their last meeting, the colonel's bitterness was certainly understand-able, and Paul would attempt to make every effort to make himself likable to the oldster.

As it turned out, Rogers had been friendly enough. They sat at the kitchen table with coffee talking about the weather, fishing, and the cost of feed. Everything but what was uppermost in all their minds, the gray wolf.

Paul spent some time giving the colonel directions to his favorite fishing hole on a tributary creek of the Bighorn River. A trophy rainbow trout was lurking there and Paul had never been able to hook it although he had seen the fish on several occasions. The colonel was welcome to try.

The Bighorn offered over seven thousand trout per mile of river averaging eighteen inches in length, making it a fly fisherman's paradise. Taylor was surprised when the gruff old man indicated he would like to join him on some future fishing excursion. He was surprised again to learn that they both were avid fly fishermen, and the colonel could talk the talk with him.

Susan drew weary of the fish chatter and finally announced their intention of going horseback riding. They had drunk all the coffee they wanted, and it would soon be getting hot so she wanted to go early. She didn't mention to her father her decision to ride north to Bear Mountain.

Pancho had saddled a well-used mare for Paul, and Susan set about saddling Little Joe. She was the only one who could saddle the fractious bay horse to her satisfaction.

She led the way, Little Joe irritated with being reined in to match the slow, plodding gait of the old mare.

Circling Bear Mountain they climbed steadily as the mountain foliage became sparse and the ground rocky. Reaching a flat bench about half way up the increasingly steep slope, Susan led them out an indefinite trail about a hundred yards and stopped. Dismounting, they tied the horses and proceeded to an open overlook that in reality was a huge boulder projecting out from the side of the mountain. It looked like it might tumble into the valley below with the slightest provocation. The nimble girl scrambled up to the top of the massive rock and walked toward its edge.

"Easy, Susan. You might slip." Taylor had been right behind her, but it was precarious and required caution.

"Look at that, Taylor," she said, finally stopping at

the lip of the giant projection.

"Whew, what a view," he exclaimed, genuinely impressed. He hadn't ventured as close to the edge as Susan and silently wished she would step back a few paces.

They were scrutinizing the panorama of at least ten percent of the State of Montana and maybe a part of Wyoming. It was breathtakingly spectacular.

The two stood in silent fascination, gazing into infinity until the swaying shortgrass green turned into sky blue at the curvature of the earth.

"It's so enormous," she whispered.

"Yeah. And we're seeing only a small fraction of the western edge of it," Taylor whispered back.

"The edge of what?"

"The greatest expanse of grassland in the world."

"In the world? Really?"

"Well, it's lost a lot of its identity, what with the roads, and cities, and farms. Can you imagine what it looked like two hundred years ago? It had to be awesome."

"It still is," she sighed, trying to visualize a thousand miles of rippling grass.

"At one time 70 million American bison called it home. 50 million pronghorn antelope. And they were the animals at the top of the range ecosystem. There is no authority that would hazard a guess on the smaller groups." He laughed, "The prairie dog numbers would challenge a computer."

"70 million buffalo boggles my mind," she said quietly.

"Do you come up here often?" he asked.

"At least once a week. Of course, now that a gray wolf supposedly prowls these parts, Dad doesn't think I should be riding up here by myself."

"Have any of the ranch people heard the wolf howl since the night Big Red was killed?" Paul questioned.

"I don't think so," she answered.

"Wolfman thinks he will leave the area now that his mate is gone. Perhaps he has already left." Paul suggested.

"Let's hope so. I don't want him killed."

"No, it would solve nothing since he hasn't been killing your livestock." Taylor had quickly rooted out the truth of the dogie kill that had started the string of events. Even the hunters had not believed the female wolf had killed the calf.

There was a long silence as they shared the magnificent view.

"By the way, we think we know where the pair came from," Paul stated, referring to the male and female wolves.

"Oh? How did you determine that?" Susan asked with interest. Not where or why, but how. The woman had a searching and complex approach to questions.

"Wolfman called a friend in Saskatchewan who's an authority on wolves in Canada. We had already discounted the possibility that they came from the Idaho, Yellowstone, Glacier, or Bitterroot packs or was a stray pair from the Northern Rockies. That left Saskatchewan. It didn't sound feasible because of the distance involved but there was no other explanation we could come up with.

"Dominick LeBare, Wolfman's friend up in Regina, said a pack from the lake region around Prince Albert National Park had been roaming out of the boreal forest up the Saskatchewan River for the last several years. Coming up the Sas right out of the woods into the grasslands. LeBare said it was the darndest pack he had ever seen, claiming half of Saskatchewan as their territory.

"Wolfman and I believe the pair may have come from that pack.

"Like I say, it all makes sense except for the distance." Taylor paused to give a short chuckle. "Wolfman said that fellow must have a foot on him. We can't believe a pair of wolves would move this far south for whelping. But if they did, it was a straight shot to Bear Mountain. Right down through Charles M. Russell National Wildlife Refuge and just west enough to get past Fort Peck Lake. Like I said, a straight shot." Taylor was pleased with his own deduction. "There are half-a-dozen wildlife refuges they could have hit taking that route. Just like McDonalds along the Interstates except they didn't have to pay."

"How did they get across the Missouri River?" she asked.

"They can swim like fish. No sweat west of Fort Peck Lake."

"But why here?" Susan was still trying to sort it out in her mind.

"Well, just look at that view. Where else would they find that? They don't call this Big Sky Country for nothing." Taylor was laughing. "Seriously, a whelping pair seeks the most remote place they can find to have their young. This land is about as isolated as it gets. Under three people per square mile. Less than that right around here. No people per square mile here, except us today.

"Southern Saskatchewan is pretty heavily populated, relatively speaking, so maybe it shouldn't be a surprise the pair traveled so far south." Taylor was convinced he had figured it all out.

"Perhaps they have been coming here a long time.

Nobody ever comes up on this mountain except me. . . . and my friends," Susan added warmly.

Taylor had been deep in thought and had missed the kind remark.

"LeBare told Wolfman something else interesting. He said the pack identification for the last fifteen years or so has been the alpha male. The wolf is coal black and almost twice the size of the other male members." He grinned. "Those Canadians are uniquely descriptive of their wildlife. LeBare, without humor, said the alpha male had legs like stilts, feet like snowshoes, and could outrun lightning."

"That sounds doubtful in more ways than one. No wolf is going to live that long, let alone be the alpha male for fifteen years," Susan responded logically.

"Yeah, but it could be a succession of offspring. A look-alike son who takes over from his father."

"A-ha! Back to my hot genetics theory that you tried to dowse with leaky logic," she asserted.

"I plead innocent," he laughed. "But you have me in a corner, and I want to change the subject."

"Before you do, I have a couple more questions since we are discussing the wolf.

"From what I read in the paper, there is a lot of opposition to the reintroduction program. Why are so many folks against it?" She hadn't paid much attention to the almost daily articles until wolves had touched her own life.

"Oh, a variety of fears, attitudes, misinformation, ideological differences, distrust in government, born aginners. Some are not against the establishment and protection of wolves in order to maintain a naturally occurring wildlife ecosystem. They simply believe we should let the wolves proliferate on their own and let the ecosystem develop without us tinkering with it.

"The problem with that approach is time. Our grand-children would not live to see it happen. Wolves cannot and will not migrate freely and safely down into Wyoming and Idaho because of human pressure. Man has gotten in the way of safe passage for them. The No Return wildlands in central Idaho can probably sustain wolves, but it's up to us to put them there. Same with Yellowstone. Actually, there is such an abundance of ungulates in Yellowstone that a viable wolf population shouldn't even make a dent in them.

"In other words, we have to jump start this ecosystem to help it happen. Once we can approximate a balance, then Mother Nature will have a chance to adjust it and keep it going." Taylor found himself enjoying expressing his views to this unbiased lady.

"Sounds neat and orderly to me. But I guess there are a lot of people like Dad. It's the way they were brought up." Susan said.

"We have evidence now that the wolves we have already released in Yellowstone are reducing the coyote population there considerably. That should placate the hard-line ranchers like your father."

"I doubt it. Dad will never change. He's too old to start altering his convictions. People like Dad don't listen. They already know." She recognized how morbid she sounded, and she wanted to change the subject too. Her pensive mood brightened. "Now what did you want to talk about?"

He had been standing behind her not willing to move as close to the brow of the overlook as she had. "You are still calling me Taylor," he stated in a low voice.

Suddenly she turned, almost against him. She

smiled up into his eyes, her full red lips within inches of his reach. "I happen to like Taylor," she breathed softly.

Then they were touching, Paul was kissing her, and she was against him hard. Every nerve ending in his body was on fire. Her lips were quivering against his own, and he felt the electric shock of the tip of her tongue.

Tightening his arms, he could feel her entire length burn into his embrace and then it was over. She pulled back breathlessly. "Taylor, I . . . ."

"What's the matter?" he croaked.

Pulling herself up straight, she took a deep breath and was back in control of her emotions.

"We need to talk. Let's go back."

****

The food was good, but the rejection had spoiled his appetite. Susan's cooking talents were apparent as he watched her moving about the kitchen in complete control. Then he remembered she had been away on her own for several years. College, medical school and then practicing for a year. Learned to cook from necessity, probably. Or maybe from her mother or Rozita.

They ate almost in silence, and if the colonel had not been chattering away, the tension would have been conspicuous in the room. It was over an hour before the table was cleared, the dishes in the dishwasher, and the colonel had excused himself for the luxury of an afternoon nap.

She started the conversation with a straightforwardness that surprised him.

"Taylor, I had an affair with a married man. As a matter of fact, he had a child. Maybe children. It was more than an affair. I lived with him for six months. More correctly, he lived with me. He was a young doctor finishing his internship at Bellwood Memorial in Chicago, where I was on the obstetrics staff."

Paul sat listening to her words and starring blankly at the now barren kitchen table.

"After I found out he was married, I ended it, of course. I found out there was also another woman he was seeing as well as me. The entire lurid affair was so revolting I wasn't sure I would survive it.

"Dad doesn't know it, but that was the real reason I resigned my position and returned home. It just happened to coincide with Mom's death, and he thought I was coming back home to care for him. I pray he never finds out the truth." She had paused to choose her next words.

"What's that got to do with us?" he blurted.

She looked at him with an expression of anguish. "Everything. I don't think I could make a commitment again this soon. I'm just not ready for it. And it's something you should know about. I would feel guilty hiding it."

"Hell, I'm not asking you for a commitment. Men are like apples, Susan. Every now and then you bite into a rotten one. That shouldn't turn you against apples, should it?" He was beginning to get upset. The revelation had stunned him. Was she fearful that he was like the weasel who took advantage of her? Or was this a way to keep him at arms length?

"I guess not, but I can't help the way I feel. Maybe you could be patient with me. I believe you are a very understanding person."

"Understanding? I sure don't understand this. So you got involved with a married man and a womanizer, and you were grievously hurt and offended. I'm sorry it happened to you, but it shouldn't be the end of the world. All that had to have occurred over a year ago. You need to get on with your life." He stopped talking, as if another thought had sprung into his head. "Gee, all I did was kiss you. Does that call for complete rejection? You sure it's not something else?" Taylor was getting angry, something he rarely did. He had worried about the obstacles between them ever since she had stolen his heart the moment she had opened the front door that fateful day and had smiled up at him. He had conjured up every conceivable hurdle that might confront them, but he had never dreamed it would be something like this.

"You think I might be like that creep?" He was shouting now.

"No, of course not. And I wasn't rejecting you. I just wanted you to know I've had a hard time dealing with this," she said quietly.

"Who don't you trust, me or yourself?" he snapped.

She started to say something, but Taylor kept talking. Accusingly and in a low voice, he continued. "What it really is and maybe you don't even see it, but what it really is all about is the social and economic chasm separating us, isn't it? I'm simply not in your league. I'm not good enough for a Rogers. I'm only a common public servant paid to provide a service for people like you."

Susan interrupted him with a loud cry. "No, of course not." Her face was pale and contorted in disbelief. They were the most hateful and caustic words she had ever heard. How could this pleasant, gentle man suddenly be saying such things?

He hadn't heard her. "I knew it would come to this.

That it wouldn't work. It was destined for failure from the very beginning." Taylor had risen from his seat, anger across his features.

"Well, thanks for the chicken dinner. I guess you do know how to come down and mingle with the common folk occasionally." Turning, he fled through the house and out the front door.

He heard her scream his name behind him, and then he was driving down the dusty gravel lane at a neck breaking speed.

The car slowed, the narrow road becoming blurry. There had been few spells of this in his adult life. A grown man, he thought, as he made a swipe across his eyes with the back of his hand.

God, that woman had gotten to him.

CHAPTER IX

Wolf watched the two horseback riders from his position on the grassy knoll near the ranch. They had ridden out from the dwellings in the direction of the high mountain. Wolf felt no apprehension because they were not hunters, and he lazily watched them disappear in the distance. He noted one of the riders was the female two-legs.

The knoll was where he spent most of his time since the encounter with the dogs. The matted hair and coagulated blood on his right flank was the aftermath of that terrible fight. The fight that he wouldn't end until the evil dogs that had killed his babies were dead themselves. The enmity between wolf and dog was as old as life itself, but Wolf's hatred of the Rogers dogs went far beyond the normal animosity between the two species.

He had received several puncture wounds and lacerations around his face and through his shoulders, but it was the deep cut on his right hip which was the most troublesome. Painful and debilitating, it caused him to seek out the soft, grassy spot near the clear, cool stream where he could drink and sometimes lie in the soothing waters. The coldness would quiet the throbbing ache and ease the fever in his body.

Climbing up and down the steep parapets of the distant mountain had been too difficult and agonizing. At night he could pounce on an occasional hare near the water when they would come to drink or perhaps a swimming muskrat. He needed rest in order for the wound to heal and lying in the clean grass without movement made the pain endurable.

It was safe enough. There were no dogs now at the two-legs' place, and he would quickly know if new dogs were brought in. But the primary reason he had been drawn to the sundrenched rise was the view of the two-legs' shelter. The female two-legs had emerged every day from the rear of the stone structure with the small, white wolf baby. They would roll playfully in the grass until she tired, and then the puppy would be taken back inside.

Wolf now knew where the remainder of his young family was, although the white baby was the only one he had seen.

Intending to move north after the planned confrontation with the two-legs' dogs, Wolf would now be forced to wait until he had recovered sufficiently to make the journey. He had not reckoned on the additional dogs that had been brought in for the chase. Only by great resolve had he accomplished his goal, and it had been done at great sacrifice. He was quite vulnerable now, and his salvation rested on the two-legs not bringing in more dogs. If another hunt was organized, he would be forced to leave quickly, and if they found his trail, he would have great difficulty outrunning them.

But he wouldn't run until it was absolutely necessary.

Some little understood compulsion dictated he stay. Even had he not been injured, he would have been hopelessly bound to the commanding view he had discovered. It was a place where he could sometimes see his offspring and be comforted with the knowledge that she was all right.

His heart had leaped when he first saw the young wolf with the female two-legs. There had been many strange odors during his brief incursion into the two-legs' domain, but there had been no scent of his babies. He had worried about it constantly and the relief was heady.

Abandoning the remnants of his family now was too heartrending to contemplate. Had he been capable of traveling to the north country, he could not have done it. The north pack would not need him until the white rains came, and the long trek north could not be safely made until he healed. There was plenty of time for that, and he could travel slowly. It was still the time of the prairie flowers, and the white rains would not come soon. When his wound had healed, he would go. The core pack would be there, and they could provide food of substance again. A deer or young elk. No more rabbits and field mice.

Being delayed on his return to the north country because of his injuries was not particularly distressing to Wolf. Under ordinary circumstances he would not have started the long journey with a new family until the nights turned cold anyway. The delay would allow him more time to watch his own and contemplate their return to the wild lands where they belonged. He wasn't worried that the gray wolves would become dependent on the two-legs like the detestable dogs. They were of his blood and of his mind. They would run with him someday. He was sure of it.

Wolf was drawn from his reverie by the two horseback riders returning. The one accompanying the female two-legs was the visitor who had come earlier in the noisy rolling thing. Maybe the female two-legs would bring the young wolf outside again since it was only midday.

Wolf waited patiently. When the tall two-legs came outside and hurriedly went away in the dark rolling object, he anticipated seeing the white wolf come out of the house.

It didn't happen although Wolf held his vigil until the shadows of dusk obscured his vision. The frustration was crushing. It was the first day since the lonely watch began that the little female had not been brought outside the dwelling. The disappointment stimulated his memory of his own first days of life. When he had been only slightly older than his own young he was so eager to see.

Wolf had little memory of his mother, but he could remember vividly the large bone she had brought him specifically. As if she had favored him over all the others in the litter. It brought on the first responsibility of protecting what was his own. He would have died rather than let any of his brothers take the bone from him, and his fierceness began developing at an early age.

The bone became his security blanket, and he had slept with it gripped tightly between his legs.

It had also developed his jaws and sharp white teeth as he idled time away chewing incessantly on the stark white hardness. It had long before given up any hint of flavor or nutrition, but a primal need to attack the coveted possession was constantly with him.

A final lesson had been learned from the old bone. He had dragged his treasure outside the lair one day in order to play in the warm sun. An adult wolf had watched the youngster frolicking and without warning had dashed in and snatched the bone which had been left temporarily un-guarded.

Wolf had been on the culprit in a split second, and the older wolf had bitten him painfully across the bridge of the nose. It was one of the few times in his life that he had retreated from a fight, and it had never been forgotten.

Later, Wolf would come to the realization that the lesson learned was far more important than losing the cherished bone. That bravery and foolishness were not synonymous. That a wise wolf knew when to retreat. And a clear understanding that his most important assets were his feet and not his teeth. That lesson had sustained Wolf for many years and was always uppermost in his mind when confronted with danger.

Wolf's massive jaw muscles and great physical endurance had developed as he grew, and in his mind it had all been because of that first possession. Like the remembrance of a good friend of loved one, he could still picture the tooth-marked, white bone. Although he couldn't remember his mother, there was an underlying awareness that she had done her job well.

After fatigue finally won out over the dull ache in his flank and he slept that night, he dreamed of the white female. In the dream she had brought a large white bone to her litter, and there had been a struggle for possession of it among the five babies.

Unexpectedly, the smallest, the baby white female captured the bone with a fierce intensity not unlike her mother's when she was growing up. The little white female would be exactly like her mother, and Wolf would protect her to his dying breath.

CHAPTER X

The summer drifted lazily along. June and July were hot and dry with temperatures in the eighties almost every day. It was too hot to ride except very early in the mornings, so Susan kept Little Joe exercised by taking short jogs around the confines of the ranch environs. She longed for a jaunt into the mountains, but the colonel continued to be adamant in his refusal to let her go. She was a grown woman, and it would have been easy to disobey him, but she had not been reared that way. The assault on her conscience would have been far more disturbing than a tongue lashing from her father.

She recognized he was not trying to exercise control over her private activities. It was simply fatherly concern over her well-being, and she didn't wish to worry him unnecessarily.

Gray Girl was growing, and every morning before the heat became uncomfortable they would play together in the soft grass of the backyard. The wolf's training had reached a point where Susan had begun to lead her around the ranch complex, and it had become a topic of conversation among the ranch hands. They avoided the growling wolf like the plague, and Susan was the only one who could safely handle her.

Colonel Rogers had become reconciled to the presence of the young animal. The guilt he felt from the loss of the dogs prevented him from objecting openly to Susan's avid project.

The gray wolf hadn't been heard since the night of Big Red's death over two months earlier. Of course, the demise of the other two dogs the following day also was attributed to the wolf although no one had seen it happen. No one had witnessed the animal attacking Big Red either.

There had been much speculation as to why the lone wolf had not howled the night after Max and Beethoven were killed. Triumphant echoes of his howls had reverberated throughout the sky the night before when Big Red died. None could have known of the gray wolf's injuries that had dictated the silence the following night.

It had been puzzling to all but Billy Greateyes. Billy's eyes were all-seeing and knowledgeable. None of what had happened had perturbed him. When the hands would grumble about the young wolf being led around the ranch by the woman doctor, he would offer words of great import.

"According to Blackfeet tribe, wolves were already in existence when human beings were created. Since only the old are wise, the wolf brothers taught the young mortals how to live with all the beasts. Then the young mortals forgot what they had learned because they were not old enough to be wise."

Or he might say, "The wolf is our fellow traveler through life. When the wolf father calls, it is to share the great horned beasts with us so there is plenty for all. But when the great wolf does not call, it is a silent message that we must travel with great care."

Few of the ranch workers took him seriously, especially Cody Watkins who was openly hostile toward the old Indian. Yet, Billy never took umbrage over Watkin's unkind retorts which tended to make the curly-haired cowboy even madder.

So with time, it all became a deep mystery story told in a variety of forms by the ranch hands. The Fish and Wildlife personnel had rejected it all, understanding the tendencies of human imagination, and if there really had been a wolf, mate to the slain female wolf, he was long gone.

But the presence of the young and growing gray wolf at the ranch kept the experience alive in the minds of all the men. They talked about it constantly, mostly in low conversation while they worked or just before sleeping while lying in their bunks.

A group of them had been in the holding corral marking and separating cows destined for market one morning when Susan was exercising Gray Girl.

"Looks like the colonel's daughter is out walking her puppy again," drawled String Starcher. The tall, lanky kid could hardly cast a shadow on a sunny day yet was always first in the chow line.

"Wonder whatever happened to that wildlife feller used to come out here every Sunday?" asked Ed Hastings, one of the older hands and a rodeo has-been. He finally quit the circuit, he said, because the ground kept getting harder and further away.

"He probably tried to feel her pulse and the lady doctor sent him packing," Cody Watkins offered without amusement. He had never gotten over his own early infatuation with the young woman.

"I'd let that doctor feel my pulse anytime," cackled old Pecky, who had been standing around as usual watching the work.

"Musta been something between 'em for him to come clear out here from Billings every week just for Sunday dinner," Hastings speculated.

"Hey, man, I don't want no truck with no lady doctor. They's got to be colder'n a well-digger's ass." String had stopped working to watch the young blonde and the wolf pup as they walked down the ranch driveway. He was watching the movement of the tight jeans. "Yet, like they say, cold water runs deep."

"Shit, String, that's still waters run deep," laughed Watkins.

"Here comes Buck, you guys. It's gonna be hot water if we don't get to hustling." Ed had grabbed a cattle prod and started separating a cluster of cows.

****

The first part of August arrived before the dry spell was broken by a series of thunderstorms preceding a fast moving cold front. The front roared through during the night, and the next day dawned with clear, crisp air producing unlimited visibilities. It would be a typical Montana Big Sky day.

"I sure would like to ride today, Dad. It's marvelous outside," Susan announced at breakfast. "Do you think it would be all right to ride up on the Bear? Bet I could see forever up there this morning," she asked hopefully.

"If you'll be careful. I guess that damn wolf is gone from these parts by now," he answered absently. The months rolling by without any sign of the gray wolf had tempered the old man's judgment.

"Oh, Dad, you know there isn't any danger. Even if he were still around, wolves don't attack human beings," she laughed.

"They don't attack dogs either. They are supposed to run from them," he growled scornfully. He clearly knew he had been responsible for the deaths of the ranch dogs and had been trying to make amends gracefully with Susan all summer. It had been amusing and sometimes comical the way he offered contrition, and Susan was careful not to make it too easy for him.

The girl hardly heard him as she bounced out of the house toward the barn.

Rozi came out with a sandwich and an apple just before Susan was ready to go. She had saddled the gelding and was leading him out of the barn. Rozi also had a water bottle filled with Montana spring water which they kept refrigerated for daily use.

"Thanks, Roz," the anxious rider said. She took the time to stash the lunch in her saddlebag and hang the water bottle over the saddle horn.

Little Joe was anxious as well. He bolted into a quick lope as soon as Susan was mounted, and the two dashed across the shortgrass field toward Bear Mountain.

Susan ate her lunch on the Susan's Retreat rock, then sat for about thirty minutes gazing across the wide expanse of rolling grass below her. The view this day was spectacular. She hadn't realized how much she had missed her mountain rides.

Recalling her last visit to this secret place, a terrible feeling of sadness washed over her. Why had Taylor stalked out of her life that way? There was no validity in his accusations. He had hurt her deeply, and she had been unable to sleep for a week after it happened.

If he had only given her a little time. She had expected his support and understanding. Why had he not seen the trauma she had experienced over the Wright affair? Couldn't he have recognized that she was baring her deepest secret to him and only wanted his help in dealing with it? He should have understood that she couldn't rush headlong into another affair with a man without being sure where it would lead. She was only trying to be honest with him. She had not known Taylor long enough to throw caution to the wind and expose her vulnerability again. Why couldn't he understand that?

Instead, he had accused her of playing games. Some nonsense about an economic and social gap separating them that he couldn't bridge. The man must be wracked with self-doubt and insecurity. He had seemed so stable and strong. She was thirty years old and still didn't know the subtleties of handling a man. She shouldn't have told him about Ray Wright. It had served no useful purpose beyond an outlet for her own guilt. Why had she felt a need to share such a personal experience?

And what about Taylor's charges that she was an elitist? That was patently ridiculous, but in retrospect she could see how he could arrive at that conclusion. She knew she had been privileged all her life, but she had never exploited the position in life which had been beyond her control. In fact, she had always made every effort to avoid that label. She had tried to turn it in a direction which would help the less fortunate. The year she had spent at Bellwood would always be in her memory as the most rewarding of her life.

The worst part was that Taylor had sought no middle ground. No opportunity for discussion. He had simply gotten mad and walked out of her life. No phone call or effort to contact her. She had called to apologize for her father's rudeness. If there was to be any more apologizing it would be Taylor doing it.

Well, she had worried herself sick over it long enough and now it was over. The emotional pain was becoming more bearable with each passing day or was she merely becoming anesthetized to it? No matter; she had gotten over Ray Wright and she would get over Paul Taylor.

Getting over Wright had been easy. It was the deed that had caused her so much anguish. The man had been a scoundrel. She hadn't loved Ray Wright, and she had pushed that knowledge to the back of her mind in deference to a normal existence. At least, normal in the sense that she needed someone to fill a terrible void in her life. Dealing with her own transgressions in that sorry affair had proven to be the hard part.

Taylor was another matter. Would she ever fully recover? Her practical sense said yes, but her heart said no. She had fallen in love with the tall, dark biologist, and that was something she couldn't turn on and off like a faucet. Taylor had produced feelings so radically different than those she had felt for Wright. He had sent her heart reeling with an intense longing she had never felt before for any man.

Getting on with her life was now essential. She couldn't be a slave to what might have been. She had to go forward and not dwell on the past.

Rising from the rock overlook she shook Paul Taylor from her mind. It was such a lovely day, and she wanted to enjoy it as fully as possible. If she couldn't keep Taylor out of her thoughts, the excursion up Bear Mountain would be ruined.

Looking at her watch she saw it was still early afternoon. Perhaps she would ride on a bit longer. The day called for it. She had never investigated the continuing flat bench out to its conclusion to the east, so she decided to ride in that direction for awhile longer. Little Joe was still eager to go.

In half a mile the bench disappeared and became a narrow ridge line. The going was still relatively easy so she rode on. Coming to a steep draw, the ridge ended abruptly. Across the cut it appeared that the terrain became flat again. It was either turn around and go back or try to make the flat across the deep ravine. Carefully, Susan guided Little Joe down the declension. As they started up the other side, it happened.

Little Joe's hind hooves broke loose, and he went down on his hocks sending Susan sliding off his rump. Rolling to one side, she narrowly missed being caught under the big bay as he scrambled to regain his footing. It all happened so quickly that she had difficulty remembering the sequence of events until everything was strangely quiet.

She had ended up lying against a slender aspen with Little Joe standing patiently nearby. The horse was apparently unhurt but when she attempted to rise, a sharp, stabbing pain shot through her left leg. Sinking back down, her back against the tree, she gingerly ran her hand down her leg. The pain was progressing and was below the knee inside her boot. As her searching hand moved down her leg, the pain rose fiercely, and she came to the shocking realization that her leg was broken.

Twice she tried to rise and hobble to her horse, but it was impossible. The agony when she moved was unbearable. Then she tried to crawl which produced even more pain. Finally, she gave up and sank back against the sapling, looking beseechingly at Little Joe.

First, she tried calling him to her. The stubborn critter wouldn't even look at her. Spoiled rotten, she decided to herself. If he had been in the pasture or paddock, he would have fallen all over himself getting to her knowing she would have a carrot or an apple. Now with the saddle on his back he knew she only wanted to climb back on him and ride some more.

Then she tried another tact. "Go for help, boy," she urged.

The big, bay horse only looked at her, indifference in his eyes. He wasn't thirty feet away.

She began throwing rocks at him; there were plenty of those lying around. One hit his hip and he jumped with a grunt but didn't take a step. Susan decided the horse didn't have the brains of a sparrow.

Worry began to penetrate her thoughts. Pancho or Buck wouldn't become alarmed at her absence until late in the day after the time she normally would have returned. By then it would be too late to reach her before darkness set in. She would probably be forced to spend the night lying on the hard ground with only the light sweater she had on. Her lined denim jacket was folded up and sticking out of her saddlebag. She could see it plainly so exasperatingly close. She could also see the water bottle hanging temptingly from the saddle horn and she suddenly realized how thirsty she was.

She tried her original tactic of trying to lure Little Joe closer with clucking noises and soft, urgent calls. Nothing worked. The mule-headed horse only stood there looking like it was the perfect time to take a nap. By this time it had penetrated her weary brain that she could not have climbed back on the horse even if he had cooperated. It would have been a physical impossibility to get her good leg in the stirrup. Pulling herself onto the saddle without using the stirrup was hopeless with just one good leg. It was doubtful she could have reached the water bottle or the saddlebag to retrieve the coveted jacket.

The seriousness of her predicament was gradually becoming clear. Susan could feel her leg swelling in the calf-high boot. The discomfort was a dull ache and had started to throb. The worry began turning to fear, and the thought of death flitted alarmingly across her mind. You don't die of a broken leg, do you? Immediately, she remembered reading about people who had died from exposure and shock. Was she going into shock? There had been a couple of times when she had been on the verge of fainting, but the spells had passed.

It was deathly quiet. Even Little Joe standing patiently nearby was noiseless. She had lost her perception of time and wondered how long she had been on the ground. The only movement was the quivering leaves of the quaking aspen she was leaning against. Despite no wind, the leaves were dancing like tailless kites in the sky. Shimmering silently, they reminded her of her own heart fluttering around in her chest.

Her thoughts were suddenly shattered by rocks clattering loudly, and Susan looked up to see Little Joe bounding down the long draw. Something had made the horse move and move in a hurry. Listening intently, she held her breath hoping beyond hope that someone was coming. All she could hear were her own heartbeats, and the only movement was the soft waving of the quaking aspen leaves. She never did hear him although it was still as midnight. A mammoth, black shape materialized out of thin air. It was suddenly there less than fifty feet away looking at her with penetrating yellow eyes. It was some moments before she knew the dark form was animate. At first, she thought the sun had cast an inky shadow against the rocks. But the steady intensity of the yellow, piercing eyes was real.

God, it was Cerberus, the mythical dog-like beast that guarded the gates of Hades. She wanted to scream, but there was no breath. Could it be her imagination brought on by trauma? An hallucination, maybe. But closing her eyes and then looking again didn't make it go away.

It looked to be as big as a bear, but it was no bear. The realization she was looking at the gray wolf sank slowly into her dulled awareness. Her frantic efforts to breathe were causing her to hyperventilate, and she was becoming light-headed. She was recalling *Le Loup Noir*, The Black Wolf, from her college days, and the chill that ran through her body made her so weak she could hardly hold herself erect against the tree trunk.

The chill turned into a hot sweat. "Please, dear God, don't let me die this way," she prayed to herself. "Take me, but not like this." Fighting against the light-headedness, she willed herself to stay conscious.

The beast was ferocious-looking. Black, with a white muzzle that made him look like a mad dog, a long, hairless scar stretched across his flank giving him a battle-worn appearance. It only added to his brutal, demonic look. The staring, yellow eyes gripped her own, and that was when she noticed a strange thing. The eyes were soft and nonthreatening, not savage and cruel as she had first thought. And the animal had sat down on his haunches indicating he was not going to come closer.

The next shock was even greater than the initial spasm of seeing the ghostly black mutant. Stretching out his neck and muzzle skyward, the wolf let out the most blood curdling howl she had ever heard. Susan had listened to the call before; the night Big Red had died, but coming from fifty feet away made her hair stand on end. The pain in her leg was forgotten and all she could feel was a loud pounding in her head which must have been her pulse. An unimaginable fear washed over her setting up a shivering over her entire body. She couldn't stop the chattering of her teeth.

Watching her for a few moments, the wolf raised his head and howled again. The call was lingering and woeful. Susan wanted to shut her eyes and clasp her hands over her ears. She couldn't bear it a minute longer. It had to be shut out of her head.

Yet strangely, she couldn't take her eyes off the shaggy creature. Some perverse magnet was welding their eyes together, preventing her from looking away and requiring that she suffer his ominous, hypnotic gaze.

Suddenly, the reality hit her like a Mack truck. The gray wolf was calling for help. He was trying to help her. For months the wary old warrior had been silent, and now he was letting the entire State of Montana know where she was in order that she could be rescued. It had to be thus. What other explanation could there possibly be? He had been on the mountain all this time, and no one had known. Now he was breaking his code of silence to help her. Even in her unsteady mental state the truth of what he was doing was without doubt in her mind.

There was no indication of aggressive behavior. No assertion of dominance so common among wolves. He wasn't coming closer. There was no other explanation for it. The wolf was trying to help her, pure and simple.

Why was he doing this? Humans had killed his mate and destroyed his family. Had tried to kill him. What kind of animal was this? Why would he be doing this? The question repeatedly floated across her mind as if she were counting sheep even though she was valiantly trying to stay awake.

****

When the first melodious wolf call drifted faintly across the skies of Rogers Ranch, several people heard it. Buck Dawson turned to the other hands working on a cattle chute in the ranch loading area.

"Any you boys hear that?" he asked evenly.

All work ceased as every cowboy listened intently. The lonesome wail rolled across the compound again, long and plaintive.

"Jesus, in broad daylight too," screeched String Starcher.

The imperturbable Indian sitting nearby began droning in a sing-song voice. "The elders say silence is death. The wolf call is for life." The chant from the old Blackfeet was as startling as the wolf howl had been.

"I knowed it. I knowed it," rasped old Pecky, who, as usual, had been standing around watching the activity. "I knowed that lobo was still around."

"Well, dang it, Pecky, if you knowed it why didn't you

tell the rest of us," drawled Dawson. He had dropped his hammer and was making his way toward the stone house.

The howl came again before he reached the house, distinct now and with greater intensity. "What the hell could the dang thing have killed this time?" passed through Buck's lips in a mumble as he burst into the kitchen without knocking. Rozi, who had been cleaning cabinets almost fell off the chair she was standing on.

"Get the colonel," Buck demanded. "Don't ask me no fool questions, woman, just get him."

It didn't take long.

"What's going on Buck?" Rogers asked, sauntering into the kitchen leaning heavily on his cane. The colonel had become dependent on the cane in recent months.

"Come outside, Colonel. I hope you can hear this." Dawson knew his boss didn't hear well.

By the time they had gotten outside, Pancho and a few of the other men had gathered in the backyard.

"He ain't stopped yet, Buck," observed Cody Watkins.

It got quiet enough to hear grasshoppers chewing, and then the melancholy call drifted in again.

"Man, something done pulled that feller's chain," chortled Watkins.

The colonel heard it too. "My God, Buck, Susan's up there somewhere. Do something, man, do something," he shrieked.

Buck Dawson hadn't become foreman of Rogers Ranch just because he could punch cows. He knew how to react in emergencies and operate under pressure.

"Get the colonel back in the house, Pancho. Cody, Ed, String, saddle your horses. Whit, get my horse saddled up." Buck had already rushed back in the kitchen ahead of

Pancho and the colonel. "Rozita, get me a warm blanket and a thermos of that hot coffee." He had spotted the coffee pot on the stove.

The colonel had struggled back into the house. "Colonel, let me have your 30-30 and some shells. I ain't got no time to get mine."

"It's in the gun case, Buck. You'll have to get it." The colonel could only sit down heavily at the kitchen table.

The revelation that Susan was on the mountain horseback riding had gone through Buck like an electric shock. He knew she had gone out riding but thought she had been restricted to the cattle range. In his mind the wolf call spelled evil. He was recalling the same howls the night Big Red died. If anything happened to Miss Susan it would kill the old man and just about kill him too.

In five minutes the four horsemen were galloping across the north field in a cloud of dust. The wolf calls were still assailing their ears as they headed for Bear Mountain.

All had heard the old Indian's liturgical chant when the howling began, but none had paid attention to the words. "Silence is death. The wolf call is for life."

****

It had been about two hours since the pleasant days horseback ride had turned into a painful nightmare, and the sun was dipping in the west. Despite the time of year, it was getting cold due to the passing of the cold front and the approaching twilight. Susan hugged her sweater around her. The rocks on which she was sitting were sharp, and she had tried to dislodge the most cutting ones, but her seat on the hard ground had become extremely uncomfortable.

A WOLF CALLED MOTKA

Her leg had swelled tight in her boot and was throbbing with an excruciating intensity. It was impossible to get in any position that softened the sharp stabs of pain. She was becoming extremely tired and having difficulty keeping her eyes open. The broken leg combined with the stress of the sudden appearance of the huge, black animal had weakened her. Although fear of the great wolf had passed, the shock of the animal had taken its toll.

She sensed the wolf was getting tired as well. His calls were coming less frequently and didn't possess the full throttle volume with which he had started. But he certainly wasn't giving up, and after two hours there was no indication of a slow down in his resolve.

Wanting him to know she was no threat, she had uttered a few words to the wolf, soft and conciliatory. What a silly thing to do, she thought. He had looked at her with disdain, so she had stopped. It had only made her feel more insignificant and vulnerable.

Looking at the magnificent creature, she could tell he was quite old. In addition to the gray muzzle, gray hairs were invading his dark, shaggy coat. The wisdom in his eyes also revealed the secret of his advanced years. Most wolves probably didn't live very long in an environment populated by humans. However, this was no ordinary wolf. With his ferocious-looking gray muzzle, the ugly, hairless slash on his flank, the burning yellow eyes and unbelievable size, Susan was looking at the epitome of survival of the fittest.

For some inexplicable reason tears began streaming down her cheeks. She wasn't crying because of her own miserable state of affairs nor because of her pain and discomfort. Her compulsive weeping was brought on by a sudden reoccurring sense of injustice. It had been attacking her conscience with disturbing regularity ever since she had first seen the defenseless baby wolves. All the wrongs of the world were being reflected in the inscrutable yellow eyes before her. Innocence lost, this majestic animal had a depth few humans would ever comprehend. She was thinking of the senseless killing and maiming of those that could not fight back. Life that could only be lived through hardship, fear and pain. No alternative. Individuals whose only blessing in life was not in being born, but in reaching that final eventuality of death. Blessed death. Why did unfairness only afflict the less fortunate? The question only made her cry more.

Perhaps the stress of her situation was crippling her with a vulnerable anxiety, exposing her weaknesses and obsessions. She only knew those glaring eyes that never left her own were making her feel a guilt the likes of which she had never known.

She couldn't stop the tears.

****

A distant shouting reached her ears and stopped her sobbing. She wiped her eyes on her sweater sleeve and looked for the great wolf. He had disappeared like fog.

"Up here, up here," she yelled with all her strength.

They must have heard her because shortly she detected the clopping of horses' hooves on the rocky mountainside.

Her memory was vague from that point on. Buck Dawson's face and the men wrapping her in a blanket were remembered and there was a period of bouncing and great pain in her leg. Whether she had lost consciousness or had fallen asleep, she couldn't be sure. There had been her father and Pancho and she could recall riding in a car stretched out in the back seat. Then faintly, the white uniforms of nurses and doctors and the smells she remembered so well from her medical years.

All those memories had formed in her brain with little coherence or order, and she was remembering them only in short flashes of recollection.

But one memory had seared her soul with rectitude and an unequivocal truth. It was the yellow eyes which had told her so much and would be with her the rest of her life. Eyes that had withered her smug, orderly overview of life and reduced it to the common denominator of all creatures, great and small.

In the jumble of remembrance also persisted the face of Taylor. How he had managed to penetrate her fleeting bursts of thought was as unclear as the other blurry events of the accident.

CHAPTER XI

Taylor had been listening to the evening news and outlining some work on his laptop computer at the same time. It was a practice he regularly indulged in because he felt it kept his mind flexible. When the telephone rang, there was an impulse to add a third dimension and try for multiple comprehension. Thinking better of it, he laid the laptop aside, muted the TV with the remote, and answered the phone.

"Is this Paul Taylor?" The voice was immediately recognized by Taylor as the deep, gravely speech of Colonel Rogers.

"Yes, Colonel." Paul waited with alarm knowing the colonel would never have called him unless something of extreme importance had occurred.

"Mr. Taylor, I'm at St. Vincent Hospital. Susan fell off her horse this afternoon. I had a feeling you might want to know," the old man said in slow, drawn out words.

Taylor's blood turned to ice.

"How is she? I mean, is it serious?" The news had

stunned him into almost a complete lack of words.

"I called Bob Cary before we brought her in. He's our family physician. He's with her now. The preliminary report is a broken leg, mild shock, and exposure. Barring complications, she's going to be all right according to Bob."

"I'll be right there, Colonel."

In moments he was weaving in and out of traffic on Grand Avenue toward the hospital. All he had done was put on his shoes and tucked in his shirttail before dashing out of the apartment. Over the past two months he had convinced himself that it was finished between them. It had been an unfortunate meeting of two people with opposite destinies, he had concluded. The cultural differences between them were far too great, and he had told himself it couldn't work. Best for both that it had ended when it did.

But he hadn't been able to get her out of his mind, and some inner hope had clung to him and wouldn't let go. The colonel's call and the news that she had been injured had swept over him like an acute attack of sudden nausea. It had jolted him into the realization that it definitely was not over. At least, not as far as he was concerned.

The drive was short, a rush of thoughts and questions assailing him as he maneuvered recklessly through the heavy evening traffic. Why had the colonel bothered to call him? That old codger despised him. Could Susan have asked him to? That didn't sound likely either.

As he entered St. Vincent, he immediately caught sight of Pancho and the colonel standing in the hallway next to the ground floor waiting room. Rogers was stooped and leaning heavily on his cane. He looked considerably older than Taylor remembered him.

"Heard anymore?" he asked anxiously as he approached the two men.

"Bob should be out here in about fifteen more minutes," the colonel said, glancing at Taylor and then looking at his watch. "They have been working on her leg for about thirty minutes now."

"How did it happen?" Paul asked.

"We're not sure. She had been riding up on the Bear. Told her that fool horse of hers was too hot for trail riding. Probably spooked at something and threw her," the colonel speculated.

"But how in the world did you find her?" Taylor had visions of Little Joe trotting back to the ranch without her in the saddle. It would have taken an Indian to have followed the horse's wandering trail over the rocky inclines of Bear Mountain. He doubted he could have found her retreat again even if that was where she had been riding.

"Buck and the boys heard the lobo howl. I knew she had gone up on that damn mountain. The animal kept on howling. Right in broad daylight. We all thought he was long gone. Hell, he hadn't howled since the night Big Red was killed over two months ago." The old rancher was shaking his head, mystified by it all.

"Buck and three of the men took off and just rode toward the calls. They were coming every few minutes. It was like the wolf was letting us know where she could be found. For some reason, we all knew she would be at the spot where the howls were coming from.

"That lobo devil had gotten her. I was convinced of it. Just like the night he got old Red and started calling. Probably was why Little Joe hadn't come back in. Got him too." The old man was getting distraught from talking about it.

Taylor could only look at him, transfixed into stunned silence by the unbelievable story.

"Hell, boy, you can't imagine the feeling. I stood there in the backyard listening to that awful, desolate howling that wouldn't stop and was convinced my girl was gone. Horribly gone, and that damn wolf was letting us and the entire State of Montana know about it." Tears were rolling down Rogers' face and he couldn't talk further.

It was several minutes before he could continue. "It wasn't until Buck rode back in with Susan that I realized what had really happened. Buck said they rode directly to the calls, and when the howling stopped, they heard Susan calling." The old man had to cock his head and look up at Taylor in order to meet his eyes. "Boy, that wolf saved my Susan's life." His eyes bored into Paul's, holding them like a laser. "I'm as sure of it as snow falls in Montana."

"Let's sit down," Paul suggested, leading the frail form over to a bench along the waiting room wall. The biologist wasn't sure what to conclude from the astonishing tale. It had become even more incredible as the colonel talked. The only sure feeling he had was the immense relief of knowing Susan was safely in the hospital with only a broken leg.

"Did any of the men see the wolf?" Taylor asked. He wasn't sure what to think of the phantom animal at this point. No one had seen it attack Big Red. No one had seen it when the other two dogs were killed. Only the Colby dogs jumping around and barking at the shear stone walls of the box canyon. Nor had they seen the wolf where they found Susan. He would bet the farm on that.

"Son, you ask a lot questions. Being a wildlife expert you should have some answers."

"Well, did they?" he persisted.

"No," the colonel muttered. "But he was there, Mr. Taylor, he was there. We all heard him." Rogers locked his eyes again. "Mr. Taylor, has it ever occurred to you that no one has seen that wolf because he doesn't want anyone to see him?"

Taylor mulled that answer over in his mind a long time before he spoke.

"Could I just ask you one more?" he asked.

The old man only looked at him with his bloodshot, watery gray eyes.

"Why did you call me?" the younger man asked quietly.

Turning his eyes down to the floor, the colonel replied in a halting, broken voice. "Mr. Taylor, when I was standing out in the yard looking up at that mountain, convinced my Susan was dead, mutilated, maimed..... I became aware of a lot of things I had refused to accept in my old age. Your opinion of me as a narrow-minded, old reprobate who didn't want anyone sniffing around after his daughter was absolutely correct."

Taylor started to object but the colonel waved him off. "Let me finish. I've got to get this off my chest." Rogers was determined to say his piece.

"After you had your squabble with Susan, whatever the hell it was, she had a hard time of it. That bright face which always highlighted her spirit seemed to fade away. She tried to hide it from me, but the girl wasn't happy anymore. And me? I just ignored it. Content to have her take care of me and to hell with her feelings.

"Having Susan back after the horrible conviction that I had lost her opened my eyes. You are a fine man, Mr.

Taylor, and in my estimation certainly worthy of my daughter. I want you to talk to her. If you two can't resolve your differences, I don't want to feel I've been part of the problem. If you can reconcile, I want to believe I've been part of the solution."

The venerable cattle baron grew silent. He'd had his say.

Taylor was speechless, and the silence was a loud ringing in his ears. The ringing turned into the voice of a graying, middle-aged man in white who had materialized before them.

"Colonel, we've moved Susan to a room on the third floor. She's resting comfortable. Although the fracture was compound, it should heal with no apparent visual or physical impairment. She has suffered mild shock and some degree of exposure. A good night's sleep should accomplish wonders for that.

"She is sedated but lucid. If you care to follow me, you can spend a few minutes with her. However, she needs to sleep so make your visit as short as possible." The doctor looked at Paul questioningly.

"This is Dr. Cary, Paul," said the colonel. To Cary he said, "I'd like for him and Pancho to see her also." Pancho had been beside himself ever since the first wolf howls were heard and hadn't left Susan's side after Buck and the men brought her in. Their mutual closeness demanded that Pancho be one of the first to see her.

"That will be fine," the doctor responded, turning and leading the way to the elevator.

Paul was startled at her appearance. Pale and hollow-eyed as she shifted her gaze to each of the men in the room, she said, almost unintelligibly, "Screwed up big time, didn't I?"

Each man mumbled something but she didn't hear. Paul was looking at the huge plaster cast on her left leg. It was suspended by a sling which lifted her leg a few inches above the bed.

"The wolf," she struggled, her voice sounding strange. "They didn't hurt the wolf, did they?" Her words were a mere whisper.

Dr. Cary, standing nearby, stepped forward. "She may still be a little delirious. It should pass with a good night's sleep."

The colonel leaned over the bed. "No, Sweetheart, they didn't hurt the wolf," he whispered back.

"Good," she managed and closed her eyes.

There would be no more conversation with Susan that night.

****

Eight o'clock was the earliest they would let Paul go up to her room the next morning. She was awake and picking at a breakfast tray. Prone, with her head elevated by two pillows and her left leg raised stiffly in the air, it was almost impossible to serve herself comfortably.

"Can I help?" he offered from the doorway.

"Taylor!" she gasped. "What are you doing here?"

"Helping a damsel in distress. It's all been worked out with your father. I'm getting a prescription filled this morning for an antibiotic, a set of crutches and home we go. Dr. Cary says noon will be fine." He had pulled a chair close to her bed. "And I think a little help is needed here too," he said, taking her fork and trying to decide what to feed her first.

"I'm really not hungry," she sighed.

"Then we stay in this white castle. According to the good doctor everything is contingent on your cooperation and behavior." Taylor was trying to reestablish a rapport with her without the awkwardness he dreaded might develop when she saw him.

"Do you remember last night? I was here with your father and Pancho."

"I remember your face and Dad's face and Pancho's face but I thought I was dreaming," she exclaimed.

"No dream," he said lightly.

They were silent as she ate reluctantly and then he helped her with a cup of tea. When she had enough, she waved the tray away.

"How did you know I was here?" she asked simply.

"Your father called me."

"He called you? That doesn't sound like Dad." She stated in a doubtful tone.

"He said some other things that didn't sound like Dad. You know, Susan," his voice serious for the first time, "you've got one heck of a father. I've just discovered I like him."

She searched his eyes, making no reply.

"He told me everything that happened, some of which I find difficult to believe."

The statement seemed to set Susan's mind to racing.

"Taylor," she exclaimed excitedly, "he was there. Not fifty feet away. He's black with yellow eyes. God, he was gigantic. Twice the size of Big Red, and Red was a big dog."

"You saw the gray male?" he asked incredulously.

"He came out of nowhere .... like a shadow. He just

looked at me. Taylor, you can't imagine it. He looked....prehistoric. Except for his eyes. They were gentle. Not mean-looking at all. At first, I thought I was going to die, but when I saw his eyes, I knew I wasn't". She paused, reliving the moments.

"Then he started howling. Every few minutes he would look up at the sky and shake the trees. It was eerie. He howled for two hours. Until Buck came. Then he just . . . . vanished. Taylor, that wolf was calling Buck to me." Her eyes locked his with a simple honesty that he couldn't discount.

The woman believed firmly in what she had related. She couldn't have concocted such a tale, and certainly the howls had been real enough. Even her father who had hated the wolf now believed the animal had saved his daughter's life. Taylor was at a complete loss for words.

"Taylor, I was perfectly lucid at that point. I know what you are thinking, but I know what I saw," she insisted.

"Why don't we wait until you get your strength back. Then I want to hear the whole story," he suggested.

"You don't believe me, do you? Well, I don't care." With a look of utter disgust, she turned her face to the wall.

"You're wrong, Susan. I don't disbelieve you. I've been doing a little checking on my own. I contacted Dr. Calvin Peters, an animal behavioral specialist at the university." He paused, and she turned back with obvious interest showing in her eyes.

"Peters thinks that, indeed, certain specimens can exceed the normal window of intelligence for a particular species. As you suggested when all this started. Hormonal and genetic combinations can trigger exceptional mental and physical development. That may be why this fellow is about twice the size of an ordinary wolf. Hormones. I'll bet his brain developed the same way." He smiled as he saw the brightness flood back into her blue eyes. The explanation did not answer all the questions, but it had gotten him back in her good graces.

"Of course, that doesn't answer the question of why he took a sudden liking to you." Taylor couldn't leave well enough alone. "Why he wanted to help you. It only suggests that he may have the brain power to understand he was signaling for help." He was shaking his head in complete bewilderment. "But why? That wolf certainly has no reason to befriend any human being."

"Do you remember telling me about making friends with a bald eagle when you were a kid?" she asked.

"Yeah, but that was different," he answered.

"What's different? You befriended him and fed him and he responded. He viewed you as nonthreatening. You want to know what I think? I think this wolf saw me with Gray Girl. Playing with her; walking with her at the ranch. I think he identified me as a comforting link between him and his offspring. Maybe even a friend."

"I think you need more rest," Paul laughed.

But it was a nervous and unsure laugh. None of it made any sense, and it all went against everything he had learned in college and experienced on the job about animal behavior.

One thing he was sure of; now was no time to be questioning her perception of what happened on Bear Mountain. After she fully recovered they could discuss it in detail. He might be able to get more insight on what actually had taken place if he waited.

As Dr. Cary had pointed out, there could have been

some delirium at play. Even mild shock could have clouded her sense of what really had transpired during that cold afternoon on the high mountain.

His analytical train of thought was broken when she exclaimed loudly in a voice that was beginning to sound like her old self. "Taylor, get me out of this place. I've got to get home to feed Gray Girl. Rozi is scared to death of her and there is no one else to do it."

"Noontime, gal, noontime," he admonished. "In the meantime, I've got to get some gear together for you."

He stopped at the door and looked back at her. "You have no objections to me taking you home, do you?"

She smiled. It had some of the sparkle he remembered. "Not at all. I'd like that, Taylor," she said quietly.

Before Colonel Rogers and Pancho had left the hospital the night before, Taylor had asked the colonel's permission to escort Susan home the next day. Dr. Cary had felt certain she would be well enough to go home. It had been a logical request, sparing the haggard colonel and Pancho another drive into Billings.

Around ten o'clock a dozen yellow roses were delivered to Susan's room. There was one word on the card. Handwritten in his stilted style, it said simply, Taylor.

At eleven o'clock he was back with a nurse and a wheelchair. Some papers were signed at the nurses' station, and Dr. Cary had a few words with her. Then they were outside and he was helping her in the Bronco.

"You hungry?" he asked, as they picked their way through traffic heading north. She had eaten very little of the hospital food.

"Since you mention it, yes," she answered.

"That's a good sign. I'm starved. How about a juicy

hamburger? We can eat on the way. I'm good at eating and driving at the same time." She needed more rest so he wanted to keep her in the car. They would stop at a drive-through window going out of town.

Taylor was in good spirits. In fact, he was in excellent spirits, not having felt so good in months. The burgers were delicious, and Susan obviously had regained her appetite, having had nothing since the meager sandwich the day before at her secret place and the few bites she had taken of the hospital breakfast food.

About half way to the ranch he blurted it out. It had to be said.

"Susan, I was so terribly wrong. I couldn't muster the courage to call and apologize." He was referring, of course, to their breakup over two months earlier. "My behavior was rotten, and I've been miserable ever since. If you never forgive me, I won't blame you.

"Your dad made me see what an ass I've been." A fear that she would reject his appeal ran through him, and his face displayed stark horror at such a possibility. "Maybe you don't want me back in your life. If I were you I wouldn't give Paul Taylor the time of day. Susan, I've been so unhappy I can hardly stand it."

Turning toward her, he offered his hand and she took it.

"It wasn't all your fault. I expected you to tolerate my own guilt and repression. It was mine to deal with, not yours."

"Your dad and I are starting over. Maybe you and I can too if you're willing to give it a try?" he appealed.

"We'll see," she whispered, her eyes soft and demurring.

* * * * * * * * * *

A leather recliner had been brought into the kitchen and placed conveniently near the wall-mounted TV. Susan had insisted on staying in the kitchen to be near Gray Girl. The wolf's pallet was beside the recliner. The faithful Rozi had managed to feed the wolf without having to touch her. That should not have been too difficult considering the young wolf was now weaned, but for Rozi it was a remarkable feat. Fear made her very inventive, and the colonel thought it hilarious when he saw the full-figured housekeeper carrying Gray Girl's food bowl wearing a pair of heavy, leather work gloves. Rozi saw nothing funny about it, and she had glowered silently at the colonel.

The elderly Rogers now welcomed the gangly pup in the house, speaking with new-found affection to the quizzical animal. Having Gray Girl lounging in the kitchen was a perfectly acceptable arrangement to him now, and he ignored the destruction created daily by the growing wolf.

The sprawling abode was strung out, but at least there were no stairs for Susan to combat. She displayed a remarkable dexterity with the crutches from the very beginning and required little help in getting around.

Little Joe had rambled in from the north pasture early that morning, apparently none the worse for wear. He had stepped on his reins and broken them, but other than being tired, hungry and thirsty, he was in good condition.

Buck had been standing by to give her the news when she got home.

"Buck, you saved my life yesterday. I'll never forget it," she had said with quiet sincerity.

"I'd say that lobo should get the credit for that, Miss Susan. If he hadn't kept on howling, we never would have found you. Dangdest thing I ever heard in my life, if you'll pardon my French," he said, shaking his head in disbelief.

"Thank the men for me," she had responded, seeing the growing cluster of men collecting behind Buck. She had paused and waved to them.

It was a somber crew that gathered that day to welcome Miss Susan home. The men had already hashed and rehashed the events of the previous day. There had been little work done that morning as they stood around in knots discussing the wolf calls. It was as if the two hours of constant howling from the mountain had wrung the guts out of every man on the place. There had been no energy for work. Hardly enough to talk about it above a whisper.

Even Pecky was subdued and in no mood for fun at someone's expense. It was the quietest he had been in ages.

Billy Greateyes had disappeared when the howling had begun. Or rather he had abandoned his familiar post alongside the bunkhouse wall where he had taken up residence in recent months. He wouldn't move back into the woodshed until the cold rains of fall forced him inside.

No one had paid any attention to Billy's disappearance until they had heard his strange, sing-song voice coming from the north pasture. Billy would wail and the wolf would howl. One was as disconcerting as the other.

It had just about driven Pancho crazy as he and the colonel stood outside the house listening to the incessant howling and chanting after the men left in search of Susan. After Buck dashed off, the colonel had insisted on going back outside, but Pancho wished they could have gone to the silence of the cellar. Pancho didn't know the colonel couldn't hear the Indian's low decibel incantations drifting in from the north pasture, but they were maddening to him. He wanted to put his hands over his ears and run to Rozi. She was always his refuge and retreat in times of great stress.

When Buck and the men rode back in with Susan it was one of the first things the burly foreman had asked about.

"What's that dang Indian doing standing out in the middle of the north pasture droning on like a dang idiot?" he had demanded of Pancho.

Vexed and harried himself, Pancho wasn't sure how to respond. He knew Buck expected an answer but he had no logical explanation to offer.

"I think he be giving that lobo wolf some of his own medicine," he finally exclaimed thoughtfully. "Si, Buck, si. That what he be doing."

Buck was tired, hungry and still concerned about Miss Susan who had been turned over to Rozi in preparation for the trip to the hospital in Billings. He had heard enough. Walking away and shaking his head, he was convinced he was nothing more than head man for a bunch of dang screwballs.

There had been no consensus. No two men could agree on what they thought had taken place on Bear Mountain that day. Miss Susan had fallen from her horse and broken her leg, but beyond that events were shrouded in mystery and the imagination of each individual cowboy.

Watkins was particularly affected. He swore it was some kind of omen that was going to come down on all their heads.

"If I'da known that lobo was gonna create all this

trouble I'da never followed them dogs up that mountain in the first place," he had squeaked. In his mind lurked the nagging notion that all the ranch dogs were dead and maybe next would be the hunters.

"Man, I thought that dude was long gone from these parts," spoke up Starcher. "I was riding herd up in the north pasture just a few days ago. Glad I didn't know he was still around."

"What would you'da done if you'da seen him, String?" Watkins asked.

Pecky had been silent long enough. He couldn't resist this opportunity. "We know what he'da done first, Cody. Better ask him what the second thing he would'a done."

Pecky's grin and owlish look were back, and it seemed to make all the cowboys feel better. The doldrums were gone as a muffled snickering spread through the group of men.

****

Rozi had fixed dinner including a chocolate cake, a favorite of Susan's. Secretly, Paul fantasized the cake had been baked for him too since Rozi knew chocolate was also his favorite. Rozi liked him, and perhaps it was a welcome back gesture.

He stayed after the meal far longer than he should have but the air of congeniality and comfort pervading the spacious room kept him glued to his chair. Having Susan safely back home had infected everybody with a warm happiness. Having her back in his life was doing the same thing to him.

The colonel was particularly cheerful and almost

festive. Taylor had never seen such a sudden transformation in a man's personality before.

When he did rise to leave, Susan smiled affectionately at him. "Thanks for everything, Taylor. The roses are beautiful." The long-stemmed yellow roses projecting out of a lead crystal vase in the middle of the long table were a symbol of welcome home and had added to the pleasant mood.

"Thanks, it was nothing," he mumbled modestly. He wanted to walk over and kiss her but thought better of it since her father and Rozi were present.

"Can you come for dinner on Sunday?" she asked. "I'm thinking about a beef roast with potatoes, carrots, and onions."

"Are you going to cook?" he asked with surprise.

"Of course, silly. I don't cook with my feet," she laughed. Already the color had returned to her complexion, and her blue eyes had that impish look he had fallen in love with.

The drive back to Billings had been on cloud nine.

He didn't go to the office or to the apartment but drove directly to Tony's. Not because he was hungry, but because he wanted Tony to know the blue-eyed princess was back in his life.

CHAPTER XII

The first chill of fall was in the air with the new day and Wolf hunkered down in the hole he had gradually worn into the grassy knoll overlooking the two-legs' place. An entire summer of daily watching had worn away the grass and produced the shallow depression. The hard pressed dirt was cool and comfortable. It had helped in the healing of his flank and in alleviating the pain.

Days of doing nothing more than sleeping, viewing the clouds floating by, and waiting with expectation for a glimpse of the now gangly young wolf had made him lazy. Except for the nightly foraging for food, his life was bereft of activity.

His mind drifted at will, and each time the youngster made her appearance he would be sharply drawn to the past. A vision of the white female would be before his eyes, and a stab of nostalgia would sweep over him. It was a craving for a past life which could never be repeated.

Even at such a long distance, Wolf could see the young wolf was growing rapidly. She would grow up to look exactly like her beautiful mother.

The morning was quiet except for the murmuring of the nearby creek and the shrill call of a hawk he could see sailing on the wind currents. His quests for food were always at night making his days of rest idyllic. It was the nature of the lone wolf to enjoy such solitude. It was in sharp contrast to the gregarious nature of all wolves and was a phenomenon of the broad spectrum of wolf behavior. Wolf sought this freedom from the bonds and responsibilities of the pack, yet was sharply drawn to the togetherness of his own kind. It was an instinctive desire to lead — to be the alpha male.

It was far past time to move north, but Wolf was reluctant to leave. The pull was great as the threat of the white rain grew close. He could smell it in the air, but was content to ignore it. Every day he had watched faithfully, and almost every day he had been rewarded with the presence of his growing offspring and the female two-legs. He would observe their playing and frolicking in the green grass behind the large stone shelter, and the distress and grief within him would lessen and become easier to bear.

He began noticing with interest a tightening bond between the two females. From their actions together it was clear a strong friendship was developing, and it was apparent the two enjoyed each other's company.

After the two legs had fallen from her horse, she had carried around a large white wrapping on one of her legs. Wolf knew it was connected to an injury she had received in the fall that day because she had been unable to stand and walk.

The day was remembered well. Surprised to see her riding alone toward the high mountain, Wolf had followed cautiously at a safe distance. It was for no particular reason. Maybe curiosity or merely something to do to pass the time.

Since his wound had healed, he needed to move about more to keep his muscles flexible. He would not see his young daughter while the two-legs was riding, so it was a good way to interrupt the boredom he had been experiencing.

After the fall and sensing her distress, he had been compelled to call. Why? he did not know. It had always been the order of the wolf pack for the alpha male to beckon – to summon. It had been ingrained in every alpha since time immemorial. The call of the lone wolf had always signaled the time for gathering. The young white wolf would need the two-legs and the two-legs had needed Wolf.

Now the scent of the white rain was upon him, and he could hesitate no longer. His wound had healed, and there was no longer any reason to delay the long journey north. There was no pain now when he walked and ran and his strength had returned. Free of pain, sleep had become easier to capture, and his waking hours had become pleasant. Hunting at night, he had found plenty of food which had made him strong again.

The pack would be reforming, and he should be there to lead. The anticipated traveling would assure his fitness when he reached the north country. The night before he had brought down a young antelope, and he was fat with food. The animal's remains were hidden in the cool stream nearby. He would stop there to eat and drink before starting out. There would be this one last day to watch for the female two-legs and his young progeny. Sleeping part of the day, he would start the long trek in the shadow of dusk.

With the instinct of a homing pigeon, the journey wouldn't take Wolf long. He and the white female had made the passage many times, and he easily knew the way. The rivers and roads to cross. The exact points of intersection.

He would make good speed alone.

A deep ache was in him as the time to leave approached. There was no reneging on his obligation to the pack so he couldn't stay. They were his charges and his responsibility. Facing the hardships of the coming white rain season would require all his energies and mental resources. There would be no time for thoughts of his captive daughter.

Survival in the wild required thinking ahead, not dwelling on the past. He would have to get the young wolf out of his mind and concentrate on leading his wilderness pack.

But the encounter on the mountain with the female two-legs had relieved his mind. Intuition told him she was not going to harm the young wolf. That a closeness had developed between the two females. How he knew this to be was not clear, but some kind of mental connection had solemnly linked the female two-legs and him together that day on the mountain. Some invisible wave length had traveled from her blue to his yellow eyes and had been transmitted back with a clear understanding. An inner bond had formed that they both had felt and would respect.

Leaving the little female would be less burdensome now because of that fateful mountain meeting.

It was painful, but there was clearly no alternative.

CHAPTER XIII

In late September the cast came off amid great trepidation. With relief, Susan saw her left leg looked just as she had remembered it. The weakness she would experience as she tentatively exercised it without the cast would gradually disappear, according to Dr. Cary. He had suggested a regimen of exercises, the most important being daily walking. Her own medical training would round out her complete recovery.

Sunday dinner had become a weekly affair, and Taylor had begun to complain about having to let his belt out an extra notch. It was his country-boy way of letting her know he was enjoying her cooking.

The resumption of the Sunday visits had once again given the ranch hands an opportunity for idle gossip. There were few occurrences on the ranch of significant import to stimulate the cowboys' imaginations, and they needed something to talk about to combat the isolation and boredom of ranch living. The wolf drama had certainly been one, but now that event had drifted into limbo.

Taking its place was Taylor's regular presence for

the Sunday dinner ritual. He defused most of the rumors and speculations in a unique manner. He began to mingle with the workers and in time had gotten on a first name basis with most of them. Human nature being what it is, the hands found it less interesting to prattle about someone with a likable and friendly face. It hadn't taken Taylor long to establish a personal relationship with practically all of them. Acceptance into the bunkhouse social structure evolved quickly and smoothly in spite of his being a definite outsider.

Taylor found himself enjoying the talk of the colorful cowboys, especially Buck, Pecky, and Billy Greateyes. They were the old ones, full of tales of the early days. The stories of one thousand pound grizzlies and twelve foot long mountain lions fired his imagination even though he suspected they were exaggerated. When it came to wild animals, they talked his language. He discovered he liked the rough, unpolished ranch gang and they like him too.

There were many amusing anecdotes of life at the Rogers ranch fomented over the years by the fertile minds of the lonely range men. One day Buck repeated one of the ranch favorites for Taylor's benefit.

The biologist had gone to the bunkhouse after Sunday dinner to spend some time chatting with the men. It was something he sometimes liked to do. Fifteen or twenty years old, the story was still received with loud guffaws and thigh slapping with a little hooting and hollering thrown in. There were always a few new men who had never heard the tale, and Taylor was one of those.

It seems Pancho had brought supplies from Billings, and some of the cowboys were helping unload the truck. Last to be unloaded were groceries for the mess hall pantry. "Mr. Taylor, you ever notice that big tree growing at the corner of the mess hall?" Buck started out.

"Sure. About the largest tree on the place, isn't it?" Paul had no idea what was coming but knew it was going to be a good one.

"Yeah. Well, we was unloading the truck in back of the mess hall and someone hollered. I looked up, and old Caesar, the meanest dang bull ever been on this ranch, was coming straight at us. He had broke out of his paddock where we had to keep him 'cause he was so dang mean. He was snort'n and beller'n and steam was coming out of his nose.

"Man, did we ever scatter. Most of us ran in the mess hall, and a couple of the boys jumped in the truck.

"Turned out old Caesar weren't interested in us at all. He had seen a bunch of heifers over in the north pasture and was making a beeline for them.

"After he rushed by, we all came out, and I noticed Pecky here was missing. One of the boys looked up in that big tree and there sett'n on a limb was Pecky.

"And, Mr. Taylor, Pecky had a fifty pound sack of flour on his shoulder. Didn't even know he had it, he was so dang scared."

The laughter had started and even Pecky was grinning. He had heard the story so many times it didn't make him mad any longer.

"Well, sir, we all went over under that tree, and I yelled up at Pecky and told him he was supposed to carry that bag of flour in the pantry and not up that dang tree.

"When Pecky saw he still had that sack of flour, he just let it slide right off'n his shoulder like it was a dang rattlesnake and, man, when it hit the ground there weren't nothing but white cowboys around here for a week.

"We didn't have to do no whitewashing for six months," he continued. That created an explosion of cackles and it was obvious the tale was being well received. Buck was going to get all he could out of it.

"Everything Rozi cooked for a month made biscuits." By now the laughter was shaking the bunkhouse walls.

"What about Caesar?" Taylor managed between peels of laughter.

"Oh, we finally got him rounded up. Those of us could still see."

Buck's wit fit the bunkhouse crew perfectly. It was one of the reasons Dawson was such an effective foreman.

Taylor had spent every Sunday at the ranch since Susan's accident, and on two occasions had spent the entire weekend with the Rogers. He had taken the colonel fishing down on the Bighorn River, and in spite of his advancing infirmities, the older man had managed to catch three nice rainbow trout. Neither had caught the "big one".

One Sunday afternoon Susan wanted to walk after the table had been cleared. She thought she could make it to the pet cemetery and back. The cemetery was perhaps a half mile from the main house, and the smooth gravel lane would make for easy walking. Her convalescence had progressed smoothly, and she was almost back to normal. Little Joe had been neglected for quite some time, and she was anxious to get back in the saddle. The daily walks were strengthening her leg, and she was walking farther and farther each day.

Three or four Ponderosa pines marked the cemetery and offered reasonable privacy. It was the first real moment of being alone together the two had enjoyed for weeks. After they arrived, they stood together silently. The three most recent graves were those of Red, Max and Beethoven. They were quite distinguishable with fresh dirt in a mound over their bodies. Small name plates had recently been added to the head of each grave. Taylor was amazed at the number of graves scattered about. Some were marked and some were not, being so old they were hardly discernible.

But the cemetery had been kept clean of grass and weeds and had recently been neatly raked. Susan had noted the fresh care given the small plot of ground.

"Panch, bless his heart, keeps this place immaculate and no one ever has to bring it to his attention," she said, soft affection for the old Mexican in her voice.

"Do you remember all the animals that are buried here?" Taylor asked in awe.

"I think I could recall them all but probably not exactly where they are buried," she answered.

"How far back do they go?" he asked further, humbled by what he was seeing.

"To when I was eight or ten, I guess."

Paul turned and took her in his arms, feeling her respond by pressing against him. A feeling he had craved her warmth forever came over him.

"You are the most remarkable woman I've ever known," he whispered.

Their lips met and the kiss turned passionate, her mouth moving on his own. Only the need to breathe finally separated them.

"We have a problem, don't we?" Susan gasped, leaning her head against his chest.

Paul thought he understood.

"Don't worry, I'm not going to ask you to go to bed with me. You've made it clear you can't have another relationship outside of marriage. I can't blame you after the experience you had. I don't think I could feel comfortable with it either." Taylor was smelling the fragrance of her hair and wondering if she was hearing the beating of his heart.

"And?" She pulled back and looked up at him. Her eyes had turned to blue diamonds which seemed to bore into his soul. Did she have no shame, she thought? She was giving him an ultimatum. Practically asking him to propose marriage.

"I don't know. I. . . . ," he trailed off. She had caught him unprepared and without an answer. He couldn't tell her about the sleepless nights spent thinking about her and their situation. The constant agony of trying to thrash out in his mind what to do.

"Is this the chasm thing again?" she asked quietly.

"Of course not. I should never have said what I did. You know I was upset. Both of us said things we shouldn't have," he answered defensively.

"Then what is it?" she persisted.

"Sweetheart, believe me, I'm trying to sort it all out. If we get married, where will we live? You can't live in the city. You have this business to take care of as well as your father. I can't live here on the ranch. It's too far to commute. Is the only alternative quitting my job and freeloading on you? You would be sick of me in six months.

"My work has been my life. Actually, my salvation after Carolyn died. I don't know anything about the cattle business. I'm a game biologist. There's no way I could be anything but a liability to you." Taylor's voice had a ring of pleading to it.

Susan's eyes softened briefly as he spoke. She knew full well the problems they faced and she appreciated Taylor's recognition of their dilemma. Maybe he had been trying to think things through. But what was really important to him? As she thought about that, her eyes became hard again.

"Don't you think you might be jumping to conclusions? You haven't asked me to marry you yet," she said testily. "Let's go back," she added. "My leg's going to get stiff if I don't start walking."

Their mood of tranquillity and peace while viewing the graves had been broken. The unpleasant subject of their unresolved relationship had ruined their walk. Repeated attempts by Taylor to get Susan back in a happy frame of mind were unsuccessful, and the stroll back to the house was made in virtual silence.

"See you next Sunday?" she asked, when he prepared to leave. "Thought I might cook some of those trout you and Dad caught last week."

"Sounds good." He tried to be enthusiastic which was definitely not the way he was feeling. At least she wasn't booting him out of her life. She must be leaving the door open. The only thing he was sure of was that he had absolutely no talent for courting a woman.

****

"You and Paul have a run-in?"

In addition to diminished hearing in recent years, cataracts were beginning to affect the colonel's vision as well. But his perception of what went on about him was as keen and sharp as ever. He didn't miss much.

Susan had come back in the house after seeing Taylor to his Bronco.

"You might call it that," she said, as she sprawled out in the recliner across from her father.

Gray Girl lay curled up on her cover beside the chair, and Susan dangled her fingers in the soft fur. The colonel didn't want to pry so he said nothing, but Susan wanted to talk. She needed someone in whom to confide. Keeping the anguish bottled up inside her was becoming unbearable.

For some time she had sensed Taylor's reluctance to let their relationship develop to the stage of matrimony, and finally she had forced the issue. Not proud of what she had done, his reaction hadn't helped. She had been hurt by his excuses and reasoning.

"Taylor has this preconceived notion of a social and economic gap that separates us. One that he thinks he can't bridge. He doesn't want to marry me because he would have to quit his job, move out here and become a "kept man." Her voice was bitter and a little remorseful.

"Honey, you should know what a man's career means to him. I think the boy has deep feelings for you. Don't pressure him. At least he is being honest with you by expressing his concerns." The colonel was being the mediator. He had begun to like and respect the young wildlife official and found himself sincerely wanting Susan and Paul to make a go of it. He had already told Taylor that he supported their relationship, and he didn't want to see it dry up and die. His daughter needed a husband. He wasn't getting any younger, and Susan should have a family of her own to carry on the Rogers Ranch legacy.

"Gee, Dad, I practically asked him to propose to me.

The bottom line is, I'm not Paul Taylor's top priority. If I were, he would ask me to marry him without any prodding from me. It's that simple. Everything else would be secondary. Things we could work out mutually." She gave him a mock scowl. "Taylor takes you fishing a couple of times, and you're on his side."

The old patriarch shook his head in denial. "Your happiness is all I'm interested in. I think the man has substance and character, although he can be a little hot-headed at times. If you two want to get married, I shall give you my wholehearted blessing and support." The elder Rogers had a further thought which seemed to amuse him. "I also think that young fellow is smart. If he lets you get away he's a damn fool, and I'm a lousy judge of character. Frankly, I don't think he's foolish, and I believe I'm a damn good judge of character."

"And you've never been wrong in your life, have you, Dad?" she smiled.

He looked at her wryly. "Maybe you should give it more time. Let things jell between you. Get to know each other a little better."

"I wouldn't mind waiting if I knew he loved me, and I had reasonable expectations of the outcome. It may be that we just aren't right for each other. If Paul Taylor isn't interested in marriage, it can't work out," Susan stated, deep in thought.

"Give it time, Sweetheart, give it time," her father answered.

Roland Rogers felt a surge of sadness. He had himself experienced the cruel passage of time. The inexorable crawl of time had left him with an unhappy feeling of what should have been. He had built his empire and realized his dream but at what cost? Had it been fair to rear this sensitive child in this remote, unforgiving land? Rose had never been happy here, but he had never attempted to alter their life-style to one more conducive to her well-being. He had been so selfish, ignoring Rose's thinly veiled unhappiness knowing she would never have voiced it directly. She had made the commitment with him, and she had honored it regardless of how much sadness it had brought her.

A terrible pang of regret passed over him, and he was looking at his lovely child through clouded eyes. Was he doing the same thing to Susan that he had done to Rose? Susan was so much like her mother. Never a complaint.

She had made light of her decision to give up her professional life and come home, but the colonel knew the pain it surely caused her.

Now that he saw his mistakes in life and was willing to do everything possible to make his daughter happy, was it too late for his own advice? Give it time, he had said. There was no time left for him to give, and Susan's time was growing short.

That is, if she was ever going to give him any grandchildren.

CHAPTER XIV

The winter passed slowly. At Thanksgiving Paul asked Susan to spend the holiday with him at his parent's home in Wisconsin. The Taylor family get-together was always at Thanksgiving instead of Christmas. Paul's sister and older brother had families and their children preferred to be at their own homes for Christmas. He had checked the airlines, and the routing was a nightmare. The holiday rush wouldn't make flying any easier so Taylor had opted to go by automobile.

It was a two day drive so it would be necessary to spend one night on the road. For this reason Susan declined the invitation. If she could have met Paul's parents as his fiancee, she would have gone. For some indistinct reason she couldn't tell him this, and the incident had ruined the holiday for both of them.

Paul's family history was well known to Susan. The strength of his family and their values had impressed her tremendously. On less than two hundred acres Charles and Virginia Taylor had reared three children and managed to send each through college. There had been a little scholarship assistance, but the feat was still astonishing. With a handful of Guernsey cows, they had made a respectable living —Charles with his milk and Virginia with her specialty cheeses.

Taylor had told her most of his childhood memories: the story of Sam Howell and his driving ambition to be like Sam, his job during his adolescent years of keeping the milk room clean for the state inspectors, the older brother, now a lawyer in Milwaukee, and the younger sister who was a school administrator in Madison.

His was the All-American family, and he didn't know it. She refused to ruin Thanksgiving by showing up merely as a girlfriend. It would have embarrassed the elderly couple and cheapened her in their eyes.

Men had such poor senses of propriety in these matters. She would have loved meeting and knowing Charles and Virginia Taylor. Such remarkable people and so unappreciated.

For Susan, Thanksgiving dinner at the ranch seemed empty and lonely without Taylor's usual presence. Although Taylor enjoyed seeing his family, the long drive by himself had been interminable and desolate. They were both glad when the holiday was over.

Christmas was a little better.

Most of the ranch hands had scattered, but a skeleton crew had remained to keep the animals fed and watered. Hay was fed daily during this period, and with such large herds plus the horses it was no easy task.

Buck, who had no family, was always on hand at Christmas time as were Pancho and Rozita. Most years, so were Pecky and Billy.

Taylor brought a Douglas fir from Billings the week before Christmas, and everyone had joined together for the decorating. The tree was erected in the corner of the kitchen which had always served as the center of activity during Christmas. The fireplace was kept blazing, and the glow gave the enormous room an aura of warmth and cheerfulness. The tree, after each individual had put their personal touch to it, brought the Christmas spirit to household and hands alike. Even Gray Girl finally accepted the glittering tree, although she always gave it a wide berth.

Christmas Day fell on a Sunday, and Taylor came with presents on Saturday and stayed until Monday. He gave Susan a sheared lamb's wool jacket because she refused to give up her horseback riding regardless of the bitter cold Montana weather. In turn, Susan gave Taylor a pair of insulated boots. The man never dressed warmly enough, she thought and was in the field constantly. She had remembered the first time she met him standing at her front door in his shirt sleeves with the windchill factor about twenty degrees.

Paul gave the colonel a trout fly assortment which was just the ticket to bring a smile to the old man's face. The collection came from the fly tying expertise of Dave Jones over in Hamilton and a better selection couldn't be bought.

Everybody congregated in the spacious kitchen on Christmas Eve, including the remaining ranch workers, eating a buffet dinner and partaking of champagne which Rozi poured with careful frugality. Everyone sat at the long table except Billy Greateyes who couldn't be persuaded from his stool in the corner. Getting him inside the house had been a major accomplishment.

An unusually cold winter wind whistled outside, but

the roaring fire kept the huge room warm and cozy. Billy refused to shed his Indian blanket, however, and sat forlornly with only his face exposed, his wide eyes perusing the noisy festivities with apparent disinterest.

The rush of activity and extra bodies in the room had made Gray Girl nervous. That, along with the bright, sparkling tree, made the young wolf gravitate from her palate to a spot beside Billy. It was as if the Indian were a kindred spirit from which she could find solace.

It had been duly noted by most in the room that the wolf had been drawn to the silent, immobile figure on the three-legged stool, but no comment was made about it.

Occasionally, Billy would speak and a hush would fall over the congregation. It was the season to recognize the dignity of all who might wish to be heard. In obvious reference to the gray wolf moving to his side, he announced, "All life, the elders say, comes from one source. Therefore, all creatures are connected. But wolf and man are more connected than all the others."

Satisfied that for the moment he was finished talking, conversation would resume with everybody avoiding the white stare of Billy's eyes. The Blackfeet was pleased that the wolf had sought refuge at his feet.

Susan gave gifts along with cash bonuses to the men. After a couple of glasses of champagne, Buck insisted that everyone sing. Even Pecky, who didn't know the words, hummed along loudly. "Silent Night" and "Hark, The Herald Angels Sing" were manageable, and then the continuity was broken in the middle of "Jingle Bells" with gay peals of laughter.

The occasion was filled with gaiety and merriment, and the colonel noted with much satisfaction that his daughter and Paul appeared to be their old selves. Laughing and bantering, they didn't notice the colonel watching them closely. Wondering what would be the eventual outcome of their strange relationship, he hoped with all his heart that they could work out their differences. He could even become a grandfather before he died if they got a move on. The thought brought forth a glow of warm anticipation that surprised him and which he immediately attributed to the champagne.

Avoiding any discussion of what was uppermost in both their minds was how they managed to get through the holiday. There was much to distract them and keep them occupied in the bustling household activities of that busy Christmas weekend.

New Year's would be different, and it would be difficult to completely avoid some personal dialogue on that holiday. Both of them were cognizant of the fact that sooner or later they would be required to address their problems and resolve them one way or another. Their relationship would solidify and become a rock, or it would dissolve and dissipate like sand through a sieve. It could not long continue with an indefinite purpose or vague conclusion. New Year's Eve might make the confrontation come sooner, something they both sought and, at the same time, dreaded.

As it turned out, they were spared the moment. A heavy snowstorm blew in from the northwest, and the road leading into the ranch was impassable for several days. Instead of being together, Taylor called Susan shortly before midnight, and they watched the New Year's celebration on their respective TVs.

"Happy New Year, Susan," he had whispered when it was over. "I'll be out as soon as they get the road open."

"Happy New Year to you too. Come whenever you can," she had answered, hanging up the phone. The man couldn't even manage an endearment on New Year's Eve, she was thinking, and she felt a great sadness engulf her. Then she had cried herself to sleep.

****

The winter had been severe with the road to the ranch treacherous a good portion of the time. Susan had curtailed her Friday jaunts into town late in November. Taylor's visits to the ranch had been as sporadic as the weather allowed.

They talked on the phone regularly, but it was always small talk. Taylor spoke of his irritation with the weather which prevented him from getting in the field as often as he wished. Susan repeated ranch activity and filled him in on progress she was making with Gray Girl.

Little was said now of the black warrior from the north country. It had been presumed by everyone that the wolf had left the area with the coming of winter. The hands had stopped talking about the fading events following that tragic hunt on the mountain, and Billy Greateyes had grown quiet.

It appeared the saga of the mighty migrant had finally ended, and the only reminders of those troubling days were the absence of the ranch dogs and the presence of Gray Girl.

However, not a day passed that Susan didn't think of the inscrutable stare of those piercing yellow eyes. The regal stance. The proud, indisputable glory of the animal. And the beneficent warmth he had transferred to her heart when he had helped her that fateful day on the mountain.

A WOLF CALLED MOTKA

****

It was the end of February when Susan received the official looking letter. She knew it was going to come, but she had not expected it so early. Also, she had presumed it would be delivered by Taylor in person.

Reading the officious language which started off "Pursuant to a previously executed agreement between the U. S. Fish and Wildlife Service and Doctor Susan M. Rogers, et cetera, et cetera. . ." had left her in mild shock. The letter was signed, Casper D. White, Federal Wildlife Coordinator, Helena, Montana.

Wolfman! Her perception of the man was shattered as she concluded the letter at his signature.

At first she was sad, and then she was mad. Reconciling to the fact that Gray Girl would be returned to the Fish and Wildlife people had not been easy. After caring for the animal for almost a year and devoting so much attention to its welfare, the agreed on return was difficult to face. She had fallen in love with the beautiful, furry puppy the first time she had held it in her lap.

Now the wolf was almost grown, and her shining coat and sparkling eyes attested to the care and attention her mistress had given her.

But Susan hadn't lost sight of her obligation, and she would fulfill her promise. She had never had any intentions otherwise. She owed it to Taylor who had orchestrated the entire deal as a personal favor to her. She had never considered violating the terms of the agreement.

But why had they sent her this blunt, callous letter without any warning? Why hadn't Wolfman White, who was supposed to be Taylor's friend, let Taylor himself deliver the message? And why hadn't Taylor warned her that this frightful ultimatum was going to show up in her mail? Were those people so disorganized that one didn't know what the other was doing? It was only February, and her understanding was that she would be required to return the wolf in the spring. Spring it wasn't and wouldn't be for awhile.

Taylor was out of town as usual, and it was late Friday before he returned her call. He knew she was upset. Martha had told him that, and he knew why. A copy of the letter from White had been placed on his desk.

"I thought you were the Fish and Wildlife Service supervisor. Why the hell am I getting letters from your underlings?" she demanded in no uncertain terms.

"The Wolf Recovery Program operates on its own. It is a separate entity from our management structure," he answered.

"Come on, Taylor. You were the go-between on this deal. Wolfman should have gone through you, and you know it." She wasn't going to let up, not even offering a greeting when Paul called.

"I received a copy of the letter. If I had been in the office this week, I would have called you before the letter reached you."

"Taylor, you're never in the office. That's just a flimsy excuse."

"You're right. Wolfman probably didn't think of your devotion and dedication to the project and figured you would be relieved to be rid of the animal." He was defending White while at the same time recognizing his insensitivity.

"Look, Taylor. I've reviewed the agreement, and there is no mention of a date specific for the transfer of Gray Girl. The wording simply says in the spring," she pointed out.

"Wolfman is going to release about half a dozen young wolves sometime around the first of April. He wants Gray Girl early so she can adjust to the other wolves before the release is made. Two of the release wolves are Gray Girl's brothers. It is in her best interest to be with the others for a period of adjustment," he insisted.

"I'll determine what's in her best interest, Taylor," she seethed. "You tell White he'll get Gray Girl when I decide to give her to him. In the meantime, you need to make up your mind whose side you are on. You know the effort I've made on behalf of this wolf. I didn't lose interest in her as you so eloquently suggested I might. I've done a darn good job with her, and you know it." Susan was definitely unhappy, and Taylor had a growing sense of uneasiness that she would do something rash.

"I'll talk to Wolfman. Can I come out this weekend?" Maybe he could defuse the situation. Susan never could stay mad very long.

"Bring some strawberry ice cream," she mumbled, her wrath already waning to some extent.

"Chocolate is your favorite," he laughed, hoping to get her in a better frame of mind.

"We've got chocolate. Dad likes strawberry." Her tone was not at all conciliatory.

She wasn't going to let the matter die, and Taylor was aware that he had little chance of influencing the strong-willed woman.

****

It was bitter cold, but the early March winds produced little snow. The roads were clear, and Paul was at the ranch early on Sunday.

The colonel was in fine spirits as they sat at the kitchen table sipping coffee. Susan was moving about preparing for her usual Sunday dinner of fried chicken. Interrupting the two men, she paused and faced Taylor. "If the lobo comes back this spring, how soon do you think he would show up?"

Surprise blanketed his face. What went through Susan Rogers mind was seldom anticipated by Taylor, but this question definitely produced warning signals. There had been little talk of the gray wolf all winter.

"Who could know?" he answered slowly. "What makes you think he will come back at all? The known range of the Prince Albert pack in Saskatchewan is anywhere from four hundred to six hundred miles from here. He has probably taken a new mate, and where she decides to whelp this spring will influence his movements.

"He may not leave the pack. If he does, it's doubtful he would travel this far south."

"He did before. No telling how long he has been coming down here. The dogs just ran onto his mate's trail by shear luck last year," she insisted.

There was little point in arguing with this lady, he decided, so he would go along with her fantasies. "Considering the two, maybe three weeks it would take to reach here from that distance, I'd say maybe the first to the middle of April. Maybe longer if the spring melt is late this year.

"On the other hand, if you recall the age of the pups when they were found last year, it would appear the pair was here as early as late March." Taylor was giving her his honest opinion. Something in her question had raised a red flag of suspicion in his mind, and as they talked it began to grow.

"Why do you want to know?" he finally asked.

She took a moment to answer. "If he comes back, I'm going to give Gray Girl back to him." She watched him closely for his reaction.

"And just how do you intend to do that?" he asked. "Go outside every night and whistle?"

His attempt at humor was not well received. Her look was withering.

"You let me worry about that, Taylor. If the lobo doesn't show, Wolfman can have Gray Girl for one of his Yellowstone packs. The intent of the agreement, as I read it, is to return Gray Girl to the wild. That's what I'm going to do. Her best interests are paramount in the return, and that is why I must first try to restore her to her father." She smiled and added, "And the way I read the agreement I've got all spring in which to do it."

"But in Yellowstone she will be protected. Anywhere else and she's fair game for every trigger happy hunter in Montana. Believe me, there are a bunch of those out there." Taylor wasn't enjoying this confrontation with Susan, but he was convinced she should consider every aspect of what he considered to be an ill-conceived plan.

"Don't worry, the black wolf will protect her. He protected me, didn't he?" she rebutted. "I'd say her chances are better with him than running with a known pack down in Yellowstone. Those wolves have two strikes against them as soon as they are released, what with all the resentment that has built up among the stockgrowers."

Her close contact with the great wolf on the mountain had endeared him to her. She had seen his awesome strength, the ghostly stealth, and unbelievable cunning. She had far more faith in his ability to protect Gray Girl than the theorists who ran their programs from an office desk in Helena, Montana. She wanted to tell Taylor that but decided against it.

Taylor didn't answer. Susan had always sensed his skepticism of the entire foible of the black phantom killing the dogs and then calling the rescuers to her, and he didn't want to open that can of worms again. No one had ever seen the black wolf except Susan, and she had been in shock when they found her. Certainly it was reasonable to presume she had also been a little less than lucid.

It could easily have been a phantasm. A deceptive or illusory appearance of a thing or object while under mild delusion. The wildlife expert's years of training and experience told him none of it could be so. Some of the tales floating around among the ranch workers had grown so preposterous they were actually laughable.

But a nagging uncertainty of his own convictions hovered in the back of his mind making him disturbingly unsure. What if she were right? He had seen strange things happen in his profession over the years and very little surprised him when it came to animal behavior. Like Wolfman, he couldn't give credence to events in which the culprit was more imaginary than real, yet the colonel had been right. That wary wolf wasn't going to let anyone see him unless he wanted them to.

He even found himself mesmerized by the sagacious, disjointed ramblings of old Billy Greateyes. Everything the Indian said was silly on the face of it but always held some semblance of insightful knowledge and logic.

Well, he wasn't going to worry about it. The old gray wolf was certainly gone by now, and Susan would eventually have to capitulate to the terms of the agreement. Gray Girl had become so attached to her mistress, she wasn't about to run off to meet a wolf that wasn't there. Time would resolve the matter. Taylor would only alienate himself further from the highly imaginative woman if he continued to question her actions.

CHAPTER XV

A period of mild, pleasant weather ushered April into Montana. It was the kind of spring weather that made enduring the harsh Rocky Mountain winters bearable and worthwhile. The clean, crisp freshness of a new Montana day was heady, almost intoxicating. Susan was riding daily now, searching the mountainsides for signs of the great wolf.

Despite the balmy days that were bringing forth the pristine beauty of a typical Big Sky spring, Paul was going to work every day in a funk. Nothing seemed to stir his enthusiasm, and a heavy hand of indifference gripped him. He couldn't seem to shake it. The realization that he and Susan were slowly drifting apart haunted him daily.

The long harsh winter had curtailed his visits to the ranch, and although Susan was always glad to see him whenever he could make the trip, he perceived a detached air about her. Maybe it was his imagination, but something felt wrong. It went back to when they had discussed the practical aspects of their relationship at the pet cemetery. They simply were not communicating. She had become standoffish, and it was impossible to engage her in any form of meaningful conversation if there was the slightest hint it might become personal.

What did the woman want from him? He had respected her wishes not to push for an intimate affair of any kind. She seemed to be punishing him for keeping his distance and not trying to get close to her. She couldn't possibly imagine the desire which consumed him to take her in his arms and crush her to him. She knew nothing of the warm feeling he felt every time he thought of her nor of his deep love demanding fulfillment. Her smoldering blue eyes suggested a rare sensuousness, and he had relished it in her occasional responses to him. On the mountain first, then again at the cemetery. But it always ended in disaster.

The intriguing goddess was a mystery. Would he ever learn the secret to her heart?

And now that spring had arrived, she still proved illusive. He was having difficulty getting through to her on the telephone.

Tony had asked him about Dr. Rogers repeatedly. The queries were innocent enough, but the questions in Tony's eyes irritated him. People were always prying, never minding their own business. Susan's absence from his company at Tony's on Fridays had been understandable and natural. The road to the ranch all winter had been hazardous, and she had refused to ride into town with Pancho. The mild spell of weather had invalidated that explanation, and now the questioning looks he was receiving were becoming irksome.

It was no better at the office. Martha had the same quizzical look as Tony. Nothing escaped that woman, and she had noted the lapses in the doctor's phone calls to Paul.

Now Wolfman was bugging him, wanting to know why

there had been no response to his letter to Dr. Rogers. Wolfman had cooperated with him in the decision to give the Rogers woman authorization to keep the wolf baby so there was little he could say in defense of Susan. Conversely, he was irritated at Wolfman for his insensitive approach to returning the captive wolf.

In short, he wanted to tell Wolfman to go to hell, but if he did it would only indicate how mixed up and involved he had become in the entire affair. She wasn't returning his calls, and he hadn't heard from her in over a week. What was happening out there? Thinking about it occupied all of his time. Each call he made, Rozi would tell him she was out riding. What if she had another accident up on that damn mountain looking for a ghost? Fear began to be a part of the worrying.

She wasn't just riding every day, she was hunting. Hunting for that lone wolf and probably probing into places where she had no business being. She could get hurt again.

Not being able to stand it further, he picked up the phone and called the ranch. Rozi answered, as usual, and, as usual, Susan was out riding.

"Has she been getting my messages to call me back, Rozi?" he asked. He hoped Rozi wouldn't be offended by the question but he had to know.

"Yes, Mr. Taylor, but she has been getting in late every day, and she is worn out. She goes straight to bed after she eats, and I'm sure she forgets."

Rozi would naturally defend her mistress even though Taylor knew she liked him. In exasperation, he asked for the colonel. After what seemed an interminable wait, the scratchy voice of the old man came on.

"Colonel Rogers, this is Paul. Hope I didn't disturb

you."

"What is it, boy?" The colonel sounded like he had been napping. Rozi had already told him Susan was out, and he really didn't know what to say.

"Colonel, I'm worried about Susan riding up on that mountain by herself," he managed.

"Well, I worry about it too but there's not a damn thing I can do about it," came the slow response. "Now that the weather has broken I can't keep her in the house."

"Colonel . . . ."

"Listen, boy," Rogers interrupted loudly. "I'm getting weary of these games you two seem to enjoy. I've been wanting to talk to you about it, and whether you like it or not, I'm going to tell you something.

"You need to get off the pot. If you're not going to marry Susan then tell her. That doesn't sound so difficult to me. You've had my blessing for six months. You two got some kind of problem? Because if you do, you need to get it out in the open and work it out, one way or another." His voice had no malice in it, only firmness.

"Yes sir," Taylor responded in a subdued tone. "You are absolutely right. Tell her I'll be out Saturday. If she's not there, I'll wait for her."

"Well, that's better. And I hope you get smart, boy. Susan's no ordinary woman even if a prejudiced old curmudgeon has to tell you that. I'd hate to lose a good fishing buddy." The colonel's voice had softened, but unmistakably it held a thinly veiled warning.

"Yes sir," he replied. There was something telling in the colonel's message. Without fully recognizing what it was, a chill of anxiety went through him.

Taylor had always been aware of Rogers' uncanny

insight, and the old man's sense of a rift between them was alarming.

Maybe Susan was washing her hands of him. Easing him out of her life. Perhaps she had become sick of his indecision and lack of purpose. If so, he really couldn't blame her.

The colonel was right. Hell, if he truly loved the girl, he shouldn't be wringing his hands about what to do. The trouble between them was all his fault, and he had hurt her deeply. Why she put up with his stupidity was beyond him. Her patience spoke volumes of the way she felt about him, and he had been too empty-headed to understand it.

The sweet feeling of love swept over him as he thought about her calm forbearance. Yes, again the old man had been right. He had better get off the pot before he lost the most important part of the rest of his life.

****

Taylor wasn't going to take a chance on Susan not being there. At eight o'clock on Saturday morning the Bronco rolled through the ranch pillars.

There had been plenty of time to think during the long ride alone. It took an hour and a half to make the trip if he was in a hurry and two hours if he drove leisurely. This morning he was in a hurry.

Formulating what he was going to say took most of the time. The remaining time he contemplated the wolf. Susan was confident of the animal's return. Clearly, he should offer encouragement instead of the non-committal attitude he had adopted in the past. If the wolf didn't return to the mountain, she would have to go forward with the terms of the authorization, and she would need his support.

What if he had misread the complete scenario and the shadowy old wolf actually was on the mountain? There had always been the nagging feeling of uncertainty that had hounded him ever since the drama began to unfold. It started with the death of Big Red, and the events had been problematical ever since. Susan predicted the wolf would return, and if she were right, where would that leave him in her eyes? He was supposed to be the "expert". The thought made him laugh to himself.

Deja vu, he thought when she flung open the front door and those deep blue angel eyes immediately churned his gut. The impact was just as jolting as it had been a year earlier.

"Come in, Taylor," she said with a fleeting smile. "I'm glad you came early."

"Yes, well, I wanted to ask you something, and I was afraid you might be gone if I didn't get here early." He was as nervous as he had been the day of their first meeting. Fear of his own question was evident in the high, haltering tone of his voice. He wasn't going to put it off because he wanted to get straight to the heart of the matter.

She had turned in the vestibule of the front hall and walked back toward the kitchen. If she had heard him, it was ignored. All he could do was follow the tight jeans that caused a tingling tightness in his body. It was followed by a crushing dread. Was it too late? Had he already lost this beautiful and sensitive woman?

Rozi was serving the colonel breakfast and without being asked she put a cup of black coffee on the table at the place where Paul usually sat.

"Can you stay all day?" Susan asked, settling down

opposite him.

"Actually, I'd like to spend the night if you wouldn't mind," he said, almost casually.

"Why? You and Dad going fishing?"

"No. I want to spend the day looking for your wolf. If he's here, I want to help you give Gray Girl back to him."

Susan froze in her chair, not at all sure she had heard Taylor correctly.

"I've been on the Bear every day this week. I haven't seen any sign of him, Taylor, but I believe he's there."

"Maybe he hasn't come back. If he has, I'll find him," Taylor stated confidently.

"Can I go with you?" Even as she asked she had a feeling that this was something he wanted to do himself. She was still reeling from the complete change in Taylor's attitude.

"I'd like to go alone, Susan. It's what I'm trained to do. Wolfman loaned me a book on the habits of wolves, and I've been studying it. Very interesting. I won't need a horse. I'll be hiking all day."

"OK," she said softly. "Can I pack you a lunch?"

"I was hoping you would. And I'll need to fill my water bottle."

He pushed back from the table and rose.

"While you're doing that I want to talk a few minutes with Billy. I also want to get my boots and some gear out of the Bronco."

After he had left the room Susan sat in silence contemplating Taylor's complete about-face. It had taken Rozi's voice to penetrate her thoughts.

"Heavens, Missy, that man don't mess around. He gets things done. If that lobo wolf is back on that mountain,

Mr. Taylor is sure gonna find him."

"You like Taylor, don't you, Rozi?" Susan stated softly.

"As far as I'm concerned, he can sit at this table anytime he wants to," Rozi laughed.

Susan hardly heard her. She was in deep thought about the abrupt change in Taylor's behavior. It wasn't her imagination. He had been only mildly tolerant of her conviction that the black wolf would reappear on the mountain this spring. Now he was offering his help in finding the illusive creature.

The predictable man had suddenly become unpredictable.

CHAPTER XVI

After retrieving his hiking boots, backpack, binoculars and a water bottle from the Bronco, Taylor cut across toward the bunkhouse. As he expected, Billy Greateyes was seated on his stool and leaning against the warming walls of the building. The morning chill was being displaced by the solar effects of the rising sun against the metal structure. The old Indian had become exceedingly prone to creature comforts as he aged.

"Morning, Billy. Mind if I sit?" Taylor said affably. He knew most of the men liked him, but it was impossible to tell about the Blackfeet.

The Indian's grunt could not be construed to mean yea or nay. Taylor squatted close by in a position that would not require that they look at each other. It was always easier to converse with Billy if you didn't have to look into those unblinking eyes.

"I read in the paper that some fellows are trying to get the Blackfeet ponies started again up in Browning," he started out.

The buffalo pony had always been the foundation of

the Blackfeet culture. As buffalo hunters they had adopted the small, wiry mustangs brought to the west by Spanish colonists. The mustangs had proven to be ideal for buffalo hunting, being fast and tough and capable of living on the sparse Steppe grass which would have starved an ordinary horse.

After the Blackfeet were displaced to their Montana reservation in the 1880's, the ponies had been replaced with larger farm horses. It had taken only thirty years for the virtual extinction of the buffalo pony.

"There are no buffalo to hunt so there is no purpose for the ponies," said the Blackfeet.

Good, thought Taylor. I can at least make him talk.

"But they want to restore the ponies to teach the young Blackfeet about their heritage and culture."

"They cannot restore the ponies as they were because the buffalo are gone," the old Indian muttered emphatically.

"But they will be able to ride them and use them for other activities," Taylor insisted. "They will learn of their past."

"The ponies will not be the same. They will not have the leaping hearts."

Taylor was unsure how to respond, but Billy Greateyes was suddenly prone to talk.

"My pony had the leaping heart until he died." The Indian's voice rose. "The buffalo gives the pony the leaping heart. There can be no buffalo ponies without the buffalo to give them the leaping heart." Billy's voice had gotten a slight edge of exasperation to it. As if he had been talking to a nincompoop.

"Billy, what I really want to talk to you about is the

wolf. Dr. Rogers is hoping he comes back this spring. She wants to give the young female back to him, but she is afraid he may not come."

Taylor waited. He wanted the venerable Blackfeet's input, but it was taking the Indian a long time to respond. His legs were beginning to cramp from the long period of squatting, and he desperately wished the red man would say something before he was forced to rise and stretch his legs. The thought occurred to him that he may have gotten all he was going to get from Billy.

Finally, the Indian's thoughts appeared to be in order, and he began to speak.

"The grizzly bear when he becomes fierce will leave his own kind. The long-tailed mountain cat must hunt alone. The birds will not come back after they leave the nest. The buffalo calf must rise and follow the herd or be left behind." He paused again for a long period. "But the wolves and human beings are brothers. They do not forget their ancestors, nor their parents, nor their children. Even after death, in the wolf family there are no orphans."

Taylor noted the distinction the Indian was making. That family bonding was greater in wolves than in humans.

The elderly savant wasn't through. Taylor could tell there was more he wanted to say.

"In the moons of first memory in the Blackfeet tribe there were many stories of a great wolf that was black. Few had ever seen him because he was so dark and came forth only on the darkest of nights. But many had seen his eyes shining through the trees and around the campfires at night. And they heard his calls from the mountains far away. This great wolf lived for many moons, and my own father spoke of him during my childhood.

"No one has seen this wolf from the north. He will be black and of great size. If you go to the mountain, you will see his yellow eyes in the darkness." The Indian paused but he wasn't through.

"His name is Motka." He almost whispered the word.

A shiver ran through Taylor's body as he listened to Billy's words. The Indian didn't know that Susan had insisted that she had seen the wolf and that it was black and almost as big as a bear. She had told only the colonel and him. There had been an unspoken understanding between them, including Susan, that it would be best if the ranch hands didn't know about the encounter. They had all heard the howls, but none would have accepted the story that the wolf was only fifty feet from Susan when he did the calling. It had been best not to tell of Susan's direct meeting with the great wolf. In addition to being unbelievable, it would have only stirred up more speculation and conjecture among the men.

Surely the old prognosticator didn't know. Were all those stories and sayings, interlocking together like a jigsaw puzzle, merely coincidental? The mystique of wolves was well known to be deeply embedded in Blackfeet history. Could there actually be truth in any of it?

"You think he's really up there, don't you?" Taylor was beginning to distrust his own rational, well thought out analysis.

"The wisdom of the council elders says it is so."

It was then that Billy Greateyes turned and looked at Taylor with his black agate stare. It was the Indian's answer, and Taylor knew not to press further.

The sincerity and conviction of the Blackfeet were unquestionable in Taylor's mind. The man wasn't acting behind a facade of Indian lore, giving ambiguous answers, and trying to be mysterious. Hell, no. This Indian was sharing a profound belief with him. He was telling him the black wolf was on the high mountain.

The aged Blackfeet was a tattered remnant of terrible times in America. The white man had brought an advanced culture to the new land, but they had also brought gun powder and an unprecedented incivility toward their fellow man. The Indian's own race had been diminished from The People to savages and their wolf brothers reduced to the status of vermin. Much within the time frame of Billy Greateyes' own life. Yet, he had not lost his dignity, nor his convictions, nor the high regard he held for his wolf brothers.

Taylor doubted he would ever meet a man he would respect more.

"Thanks, Billy." Taylor rose to go, pain shooting through his legs from being in the crouched position for so long. "I hope you're right. Miss Susan thinks he's up there too. I'm going to find out."

****

As he packed the sandwiches in his backpack and Rozi was busy filling his water bottle, Susan touched his shoulder.

"Why are you doing this?" she asked quietly.

"I'm tired of the doubts. There's only one way to find out for sure. Muhammad must go to the mountain."

"I see," she whispered. Then, standing quickly on her toes, she kissed him warmly on the lips. "Be careful."

Walking briskly across the north pasture Taylor organized his strategy in his mind. He would circumnavigate the Bear at its base, then climb the south quadrant high enough to view the ranch complex with the binocs. The investigation would be concentrated in that area if he had no luck up to that point. The wolf would be prone to keep the ranch in its scan. It was where all his troubles had come from, and he would be inclined to be watching in that direction.

In his walk around the mountain, he would investigate the canyon where Max and Beethoven had died.

Although the animal might be on the mountain, it would be difficult to find a track in the hard, rocky incline. His best bet for tracks would be down low.

Fecal deposits, always a good indicator, would be hard to find even if the old fellow were present simply because of the numbers. One lone wolf. Seeing the size of the giant wolf's scat would be interesting, he smiled. Probably would scare the scat right out of me, he smiled even broader.

Then his smile turned serious. This animal is not to be joked about. He was thinking of all the Rogers dogs—dead.

There was always the possibility of getting lucky and finding the remains of a recent kill. Large animal kills were not that hard to see, and he would scan the terrain closely with the binocs as he moved around the mountain.

It was noon by the time he was moving south again. He was now on the west side of the mountain in territory where he had never been. The mountain was larger than he first thought, and there was a lot of area to cover. So far, he had seen nothing of the wolf.

Somewhat disheartened, Taylor stopped to rest and eat his sandwiches. There was some solace in the fact that he had at least uncovered part of the mystery surrounding the killing of the dogs. He had found the end of the box canyon where the fatal fight had occurred. All signs of that terrible battle were gone, but he had deduced how the wolf could have escaped. It would have taken one hell of a jumper, but the ledge was there that the wolf could have used in making his escape.

He was remembering Dominick LeBare's colorful description of the Prince Albert pack leader. "That black phantom's legs look like stilts and his feet are like snowshoes. He can outrun lightning."

"Out-jump lightning too," Taylor whispered to himself. The wolf had led those five dogs into the deep draw purposely. He could have easily outrun them. God, what confidence. Five big hounds that should have made mincemeat of a lone wolf.

Reaching the south side of Bear Mountain, he scanned the area in all directions with the binoculars. There was absolutely nothing suspicious in his scan. During the sweep he noticed the creek to the west of the mountain. It flowed toward the Rogers buildings and angled sharply away about half a mile before reaching the ranch access road. The water was rushing with the spring thaws, and Paul speculated that trout may be in the colonel's back door and he didn't know it. They would have to investigate that possibility together sometime. That is, if Susan wasn't ready to send him packing.

Taylor could see the creek was the source of the Rogers ranch irrigation system. He chastised himself for not taking more interest in the activities of the cattle ranch. The old man may have liked him more if he had shown some understanding and appreciation for the labors of love that had gone into making the vast cattle complex one of the finest in Montana.

As he moved down off the mountain, he decided to return to the ranch via the swirling stream. It was only about half a mile to the west, and there was plenty of sun left in the sky. If there were trout in the creek, he might see one or two. At the least he could report that to the colonel. The day had been a bust as far as finding the wolf back in the vicinity was concerned. He hated having to tell Susan he had failed. He was supposed to be the expert in these matters, and she was depending on his expertise. Taylor knew how she felt about experts. She wouldn't forget him being a little "braggy" that morning concerning his ability to find the wolf.

The day had started with high hopes. His confidence had been upbeat, and if the giant wolf were present he had fully expected to find some sign of the illusive animal. However, a nagging suspicion that this wolf could outwit every wolf specialist in America hovered in his mind. Maybe he had missed something.

Then again, why should he be feeling disappointed? Maybe he had put too much faith in Billy Greateyes' all-knowing prediction, and Susan's hopes were probably unrealistic. His original doubts were certainly reasonable. The wolf might never venture into these parts again.

If the critter wasn't here, he wasn't here. It was that simple, and Susan would have to accept the fact sooner or later.

Then it struck him that the disappointment was born mostly of his own expectations. He had fervently wanted the wolf to be on the mountain. Not for Susan and not for Billy, but for himself.

The creek was fast flowing and deep now with the last snow melt. When he got close there was no question that the cold, gushing water contained trout. Brookies, most likely.

A mother otter was peering at him from the edge of the far shore, only her head above water. Her demeanor displayed mild curiosity rather than alarm or fear. The three kits bobbing up and down around her were too engrossed in their hide-and-seek game to pay any attention to his presence.

He could now report seeing something, he mused. Following the water to the point where it angled sharply away from the ranch environs, Taylor started to turn toward the large stone house in the distance. Something made him stop and look again at the stream bank just before he turned. About fifteen feet away at the top of the bank the grass had been spread apart as if something large had climbed out of the creek and penetrated the wild grasses growing along its sides.

Walking carefully, he knelt down and examined the soft ground where the grass appeared to be parted. His heart leaped into his throat as he saw the distinct track. LeBare's snowshoe popped into his head. It was larger than a big man's hand. For a moment he questioned what he was seeing because of its gigantic size, but it was canine all right. The huge nails had dug two inches into the soft dirt.

Goose bumps chilled his spine, and he stood quickly, looking in every direction. He wouldn't want to meet this animal face to face when he was on his knees. Nor on his feet, for that matter.

Taylor hardly remembered getting back to the ranch, and when he walked through the back door, Susan jumped to her feet with a startling cry. His face must have told it all.

"You found him!"

"Yeah, he's here," he answered, flopping exhausted into a kitchen chair after depositing his backpack in a heap on the floor.

"Did you see him?" she asked, excited beyond belief. Rozi and the colonel, both in the kitchen, were also caught up in the excitement of the moment.

"No, but he's here," he repeated. "God, he must be awesome. His paw wouldn't fit in that sauce pan," he exclaimed, gesturing toward a large pan Rozi was absently holding in her hand.

The pan clattered to the floor, and Rozi let out a low wail which she tried to suppress with her hand over her mouth.

"Taylor!" Susan chastised.

"Sorry, Rozi, " he apologized.

"Where'd you see the track, son?" asked the colonel.

Paul noticed he was calling him son instead of boy. "Along the creek bank. Surprisingly close to the ranch. I must have walked fifteen miles today and found the track not half a mile from here. I had already given up on finding him when I stumbled onto his trail."

"I told you he had been down here watching us," cried Susan. "He has no fear of this ranch."

"That fellow probably has no fear of anything," Taylor exclaimed emphatically.

"Remember, he walked right in here and killed Big Red less than a hundred yards from this house," Susan continued. She had long ago reluctantly accepted Buck's contention that the wolf had attacked the red hound.

"He knows we have his pup here. No, he's seen his pup here. My God, he probably watches Gray Girl and me walking around together every day." She was shaking her head in total disbelief.

"Sweetheart," the colonel drawled, "If that wolf

hadn't been watching, he wouldn't have seen you ride out that day you had the accident. You might still be up on that mountain. The rascal obviously followed you." He used the word almost with affection.

Susan wanted to laugh. The change in her father's attitude toward the wolf had been quite noticeable ever since the day none of them would ever forget.

"Want some coffee, son?" the colonel offered.

"How about a shot of that fancy Scotch whiskey you keep hoarded up in your study?"

"Coming up, son, coming up," Rogers gleefully answered. "And I'll join you if you don't mind." His walk out of the kitchen to his study was the spriest Taylor had seen the old man move in months.

A heady sense of accomplishment swept over Taylor while at the same time he was feeling a growing apprehension. For the very first time, he was acutely aware of the complexities of returning Gray Girl to her father. There would be no deterring Susan, and he was afraid she had given no thought to the dangers they would face. The enormous size of the great beast had burned his mind with reservations, and the bold persistence of the animal had made a mockery of all his professional training.

But it was clear there would be no stopping Susan.

CHAPTER XVII

The plan for the next morning was straightforward and simple. They wanted to attempt the exchange on the mountain a substantial distance from the ranch so Gray Girl would not be tempted to follow her mistress home. Neither Susan nor Taylor thought it would happen, but both agreed it best not to run the risk.

The transfer could not be made in the open. The wary alpha male would not make an appearance outside the sanctuary of adequate cover. Susan seemed to know exactly where they should go.

Taylor had halfheartedly suggested that he be the one to make the contact with the wolf, but both saw the fallacy of that. He was afraid for Susan, but Gray Girl would never have gone with him alone outside the ranch. Susan would have to be present.

"Don't be ridiculous, Taylor," she had scoffed. "That wolf won't get within a country mile of you if I'm not present. He's not going to hurt me. If he intended to harm me, I wouldn't be standing here today."

Paul saw how silly his suggestion appeared and didn't press the issue.

Breakfast was a nervous affair with neither eating much. The truth of the matter was that none had slept well that night. They had stayed up late talking, and the excitement of the day's events had kept restful sleep at bay. There were few hours of night left when they did get to bed.

Gray Girl seemed to sense something strange in the air, and it was probably Susan's excitement. The young wolf had grown close to her human benefactor making her sharply perceptive of Susan's moods and actions. In this case, the wolf could smell it. If all went according to plan Susan was going to lose her young friend this day, and she was having difficulty facing it. She kept telling herself she was going to be glad. It was what was best for Gray Girl that was most important.

Horses would not be used. Gray Girl would not tolerate them, and it would complicate the exchange. Neither Susan nor Paul worried about finding the big gray. The animal would find them. The wolf would trail them every step of the way since Gray Girl would be with them.

There had been some concern that Gray Girl might bolt when outside the area with which she was familiar and when she encountered the remote mountain. Paul didn't think it would happen because of the young wolf's dependency and attachment to Susan . If she did, the alpha male would find her easily enough.

Finally, everything was in readiness. Susan started out the back door but stopped when she heard the muffled cry. Rozi stood at the kitchen sink trying to suppress her tears.

Hurrying across the room, she gathered the forlorn

woman in her arms. "Why are you crying, Roz? Everything is going to be fine."

"I don't know, Missy. Please be careful. And . . . . . bring Gray Girl back if she don't want to go with him."

It was at that moment Susan understood that Rozi loved the young wolf as much as she did.

"I will, Roz. You can be sure of that."

Turning before she started crying herself, Susan quickly moved through the doorway followed closely by Taylor. Gray Girl, not to be left behind, slipped out between their feet. Momentarily, they paused to look astonishingly at the ranch crew that had gathered. Paul and Susan were shocked. They had an audience.

The news that the legendary wolf was back on the mountain had spread like wildfire among the ranch cowboys. The approaching drama of returning the young gray wolf to her father had whipped the men's imaginations to a frenzy. There would be little work done at the ranch on this day.

They had gathered in adulatory support for the two most exemplary people they knew in their one dimensional lives.

"You be careful, Miss Susan," spoke up Buck. "I don't want to go up that mountain again looking for you."

Susan acknowledged his concerns with a smile and a wave.

She looked over the cluster of men. Mingling among the regulars were half a dozen recent hires that Susan recognized but whose names had not stuck in her mind as yet. Men came and went so routinely it was difficult to keep up with them all.

But the ones she did know were all there, and she

was quickly aware that they had been there for Rogers Ranch through many cold and miserable times. There through hard days and long days with rarely a complaint.

The young ones weren't so young anymore and she could remember them all the way back to her college days.

There was Watkins, rather funny-looking in his oversized clothes, but as good a cowboy as the ranch ever had. She had always known of his infatuation with her but suspected it was because of her ability as a horsewoman rather than anything else.

Hastings, forsaken and put upon all his life, yet ready to give his best without a second thought.

The beanpole, Starcher. The one they called String. Always ready to go and who had never shirked a winter assignment on the harsh Montana range.

And Whittaker, the silent one who rarely spoke but who could do the work of two hands.

Looking through the group, she recognized the real old timers: Buck, somber; Pecky, grinning; Pancho, nervous; and the old Indian hanging in the background, wide-eyed with the all-knowing stare.

They looked like misfits from another generation, but all were good men. Susan was sure of that. They were Rogers Ranch men. A strange mix but one thing they all had in common was loyalty to her and the ranch. That knowledge went straight to Susan's heart.

She was also certain that Dawson had spoken for all of them and a great affection for the cowboys came over her. Looking at them, she could see in their faces the closeness they shared with Rogers Ranch. Maybe even for her and her father. They certainly liked Taylor, all right. They had turned out en masse for this occasion which spoke volumes of their dedication and respect. She was proud of each and every one of them.

It was at this moment that Susan saw herself as successor to her father's dream of a period half a century old. She would have half of a new century to continue his dream, and it would become her own. She would carry on the family tradition and trust. How could she fail with such support as she was now witnessing?

This was going to be a memorable day, she quietly speculated.

****

Spring had come early to Montana this year, and the day would be pleasant. It was fitting that the day would display Montana at her finest.

Susan wore a light sweater which she could take off as the day grew warmer. A wide-brimmed straw hat, jeans and hiking boots rounded out her attire.

Taylor thought a long-sleeved cotton shirt would be about right. A jacket would be cumbersome when they began the long climb up the mountain. They would be back to the ranch before the evening chill.

In thirty minutes the two were moving across the rolling fields toward the imposing Bear Mountain to the north, backpacks and water bottles hugging their bodies. Susan had prepared sandwiches and two apples for lunch.

Paul smiled to himself when she was stashing the meager food into their backpacks. She knew so much about him. His habits and tastes. Whatever the sandwiches contained he would like. There had been no need to make a request. She would make sure he enjoyed them.

Gray Girl was trotting close by, apprehensive of the sudden freedom she was being allowed. She had followed Susan daily throughout the ranch compound, but it was the first time she had been out in the wide open spaces of the vast rangeland. The north pasture was strange, making her alert and cautious. The young wolf sniffed the air nervously, the spaciousness stirring her primal nature. Stopping occasionally to look intently in all directions, she would then hurry forward to catch up.

Paul was awed by her beauty. Outside the house she was a free spirit. Head held high with the breeze rippling her white coat, he recognized what Susan and the Blackfeet had always known. There was a kindred bond between man and this species of animal. Man's best friend was a derivative of that bond.

"All life," the old Indian had said, "comes from one source. All creatures are connected, but wolf and man are more connected than all the others."

The loud, flute-like call of a western meadowlark caused the young wolf to pause, statue still. Regal and poised, it was a picture Taylor knew he would never see again during his lifetime.

A part of mankind's responsibility to nature's fragility was following the two hikers toward Bear Mountain that day, and Taylor was acutely conscious that as a wildlife professional he bore a disproportionate share of that burden. He had always known that wildlife conservation was essential for human welfare, but the magnitude of that stewardship had never before been so graphic. Yet, it was such a simple display of life. A gray wolf in its environment. Something that must not be allowed to perish.

They walked in silence, Taylor content to let the

woman forge ahead. She had determined the most propitious place for the meeting of human and beast, and it suited him to let her lead. He had done his work the day before.

As the terrain began to rise and the grassy floor turned into rocky, rough going, he signaled a halt.

"We've got all day," he panted.

Susan wasn't even breathing hard, The woman was being driven by an unrelenting urge.

"Think you can make it about halfway up?" she asked.

"It's about two more miles."

"Sure. I'm getting my second wind now."

Her smile bordered on condescension. She had a way of making him defensive when he need not be. Hell, he was in great shape physically. He had hiked over fifteen miles the day before.

"I don't think Gray Girl is going to be a problem. She's staying close. Actually, I think she has a split personality," Susan laughed. "One minute she can be a terror, and the next minute she's as timid as a rabbit."

Her statement reminded Taylor of the untold hours Susan had spent raising the gray wolf, and the many frustrations she must have endured during the process.

"By the way," she continued. "What did you and Billy talk about yesterday? Or is it none of my business?" Obviously, she was dying to know.

He laughed. "Nothing much. I wanted to tell him about a plan to reestablish mustang ponies on the Blackfeet reservation. To teach the newer generations about the old ways." He laughed again. "He didn't seem much interested. Said it wouldn't work. Said without the buffalo to hunt there was no point in having the ponies."

The answer apparently satisfied Susan, but Taylor

decided to tell it all. "I also asked for his opinion on whether or not the male wolf would return to the mountain this spring."

Her peal of laughter echoed against the mountainside. "Taylor, you didn't. With all your animal knowledge and scientific training, you asked old Billy a question like that?" Her mirth was bringing tears to her eyes.

"Look, Susan. That old Indian knows more about wolves than I will ever know. He lived during an era when they were common in Montana. Not only that, he lived out among them. Competed with them for survival.

"Me? I never saw a wolf in my life until a couple of years ago when Wolfman had one in captivity. Don't sell that old Indian short, lady. He's a hell of a lot smarter than anyone around here gives him credit for being.

"I'm not proud. I'll take information from whomever might have it," he concluded.

Susan's question had touched some usually shielded nerve ending, so he couldn't resist needling back. "You didn't learn to ride a horse by reading the instructions, did you? I'll bet someone gave you a few pointers along the way."

The flow of laughter increased. She could tell she had gotten to him. Then abruptly the laughter ended.

"And what did Billy say?" Susan was suddenly very serious, recognizing in herself a desire for the Blackfeet's perspective. She had always harbored a secret admiration for the red man and his unique knowledge of nature.

It was Taylor's time to laugh, but he didn't. "He said the elders' wisdom told him the black wolf was already here. Turns out he was right."

"The black wolf! Billy knew the wolf was here and is black?" she gasped. "How could he possibly know that?"

"Yes, and he knows a lot more than that about that wolf. You should take the time to talk to him yourself sometime."

"Touche", she acknowledged with an expression of being duly chastised.

CHAPTER XVIII

As the mountain rose, their progress slowed and became more strenuous. Taylor was on the verge of calling for another rest when the slope leveled slightly and a trail of sorts could be seen snaking around the side of the rocky incline. Susan turned to the east on the faint path, and her pace quickened. Taylor could only follow.

He thought they had come far enough but understood Susan was looking for a particular spot for the illusive meeting. She was seeking a place that afforded cover, and that, in itself, was a little frightening. Taylor wasn't anxious to get very close to the giant creature.

They were far below the trail that led to Susan's Retreat, and he suspected she knew exactly where she was going. An unexplainable apprehension began to grow inside him. It was a mixture of dread yet anticipation. There was a feeling that as desirable as it was to reunite Gray Girl with her father, the act itself embraced a possible confrontation with an animal that could be as dominant over humans as over its own kind. The meeting could be dangerous. After seeing the aged wolf's track, he wasn't keen on greeting the fellow face to face. Conjuring up in his mind what an animal that size would look like was scary enough.

And what would they do if the mysterious miscreant didn't show himself? Certainly it was unlikely a wolf would voluntarily present itself to the scrutiny of humans. Animals didn't do that, especially wolves. Wolves typically hid from humans and avoided any contact with them. Over the past year, the alpha had proven to be quite adept at being invisible. Susan wouldn't leave Gray Girl on the mountain without some kind of visual contact, and the young wolf might have a problem leaving her mistress under any circumstances.

There were any number of variables to how this day would eventually play out. Taylor's apprehension grew with every step he took. As they approached their destination, he had no idea what the wild card would be that determined the outcome of the most amazing drama he had ever experienced.

The trail began to dip down toward a grove of slender quaking aspen in the distance. It was there Susan decided to stop again. Sitting close together on the hard ground, Gray Girl slipped in near Susan's feet and stretched out. Paul was glad for the break and they both drank from their water bottles. They sat silently, Susan having motioned for him not to talk. Was this the spot where she expected to meet the giant wolf? It was the first place they had come to which presented the necessary cover, and it gave rise to an odd excitement in him. Taylor suspected she was familiar with the dense cluster of trees and had preselected it for the proposed contact.

After an interminable period of waiting, he wanted to speak, but she continued to signal for silence. Her eyes were large and attentive, giving cause for a quick surge of adrenaline in the biologist's body. He had heard no sound, and the unknown was making his pulse pound. Had she heard something? It was similar to waiting for a trophy buck to appear. Surely they weren't going to see the wolf here and now, but the thought flashed through his mind.

There had been no talk since they had started the long climb up the mountain forty-five minutes earlier. Taylor had no idea what Susan was thinking at this point. Fifteen minutes seemed like two hours, and he desperately wanted to stand. His left leg had lost all feeling from sitting on the rocky ground, and soon he would be forced to move.

Without warning, Gray Girl's head came up and her ears pricked forward. She was peering intently forward in the direction in which they had been walking. The curve of the mountainside hid anything that existed over fifty yards away, and a thick copse co-mingling with the aspen trees restricted their vision to about thirty yards.

Gray Girl slowly rose to her haunches, a soft whine escaping her throat. Susan sat motionless, straining her eyes through the cluster of tremulodes.

The huge, black form seemed to materialize out of thin air. It appeared as a half hidden, shadowy shape behind one of the white-barked trees, only one blazing yellow eye exposed around the trunk of the tree. The contrast between the inky coat of the animal and the stark whiteness of the tree left little doubt as to what was there. There had been no movement. The wolf simply took shape right before their very eyes.

Taylor caught his breath as the reality of the animal

exploded in his brain. Momentarily, he thought his stimulated imagination was playing tricks on him, but what he was
seeing was real, and he was looking at a mammoth gray wolf
not twenty yards away.

The discomfort in his legs was forgotten, and he was
aware of a loud pounding in his ear drums. The training of
a lifetime was suddenly immaterial. As if he had been taught
a cruel hoax. That mankind was supposed to be dominant,
and he had stumbled inadvertently on the truth. That a real,
live gray wolf could confront them without provocation and
they would become the lesser species. That it was the wolf
who decided to show himself and would direct this meeting
under his own terms. Susan and Taylor's presence being
insignificant and without meaning.

All of his past doubts. The rationalizations. His
smugness in thinking the ranch hands were victims of their
own little understood fears and superstitions. That Susan's
recollections were only fantasy due to shock. He had been
so completely wrong, and it was compounding the stark
reality he was now facing.

The eye, yellow and piercing, was boring into his
own. "You will see his eyes," the Indian had said. And Susan
had also been mesmerized by the creature's eyes in her
encounter with him on the mountain. Taylor felt the cold
impact of the wolf's dominant eyes although he was seeing
only one of them. He now understood why prey would offer
itself without resistance and without a fight. Terror could
freeze the human body as well as a rabbit's.

The single eye gripped him like life had been con-
densed into a final moment of revelation. That wolf had been
here before man, and the predator species would inhabit the
earth long after humankind was gone. The thought made

Taylor try to swallow, but his cottony mouth wouldn't cooperate.

The enormous size of the beast was making his guts turn to jelly, and although there had been no sign of aggression,an intense spasm of dread swept through his body which made his skin crawl in tingling goose bumps. A long, leathery scar was visible on the black wolf's right hip documenting past battles for survival and intensifying his look of ferocity. The white, jagged muzzle of the animal made it look like a demon from hell. But it was the lone yellow eye staring unblinking, time forgotten, that had frozen Taylor's heart and turned his blood to ice.

Susan's voice broke the clutching morbidity that had invaded Taylor's body. She had sat quietly watching the black wolf and observing Gray Girl's reaction to his appearance. At the sound of her voice, Taylor pried his eyes away from the black shape and glanced at her. There was no fear displayed in her face nor in her calm command.

"Go, Girl. Go to him," she whispered.

Gray Girl's vocalizing had become higher pitched and she stood hesitantly.

"Go on, Girl. Go," Susan urged again.

The great wolf had not moved.

Slowly Gray Girl eased forward, unsure, but pulled by a persuasive instinct she could not resist. Walking slowly away she stopped and looked back hauntingly at her human friend.

"It's all right, Girl. Go to him. He's your father." Susan's urging was pleading and insistent.

Gray Girl turned toward Wolf and trotted forward, stopping a few feet from him. The massive gray wolf had surreptitiously moved into full view making Dominick LeBare's description of the animal woefully inadequate.

An audible outcry escaped the black form. The frustrations, fears, and sickening worry of a long year were gone as Wolf watched his beautiful daughter move toward him. Grown now and so much like her mother, Wolf couldn't contain his relief and joy. Something about the moment made him understand the two male youngsters were also safe, wherever they were. Unclear and without assurance, but a connection existed between him and the female two - legs which he could not doubt made it so.

The two wolves, so conspicuous in their contrast, almost touched noses. Then the dominant wolf turned, trotted away several yards and stopped, waiting for the white female to follow . Gray Girl turned her head and momentarily gave an indecisive look at Susan, then hurriedly moved to follow her father. The pull to her own species and her own blood could not be denied. She didn't look back.

Moving quickly side by side, the two dissolved into the stony landscape. It was one of the few times in Gray Girl's young life that Susan had seen her wag her tail.

Now she could run swift and free.

Her purpose in life could be fulfilled.

Swift and free—a gray wolf's heritage.

****

The silence was as the precursor of a tornado. Neither Susan nor Paul could move or speak for several moments. Finally, Susan turned her face to Taylor, tears welling in her eyes.

"Well, that's done," she whispered softly.

Taylor found himself speechless. He could only utter

a grunt of acknowledgment. The gut-wrenching fear had left him, but it had been replaced with a feeling of total inadequacy and self-loathing. All the reasons the legendary wolf could not exist came crashing down on him like a suffocating, crushing, mental burden. The sick feeling that swept over him was one of humiliation and unworthiness. Although he had seen the massive footprint the day before and knew the wolf was real and on the mountain, it had taken the event they had just shared to bring reality to his mind set. He had been so terribly wrong. Seeing the wolf only twenty yards away had brought his error forcefully home, unequivocally and without the slightest of doubts.

But more importantly was the remarkable readiness with which Susan had let Gray Girl go. The woman's strength and capacity for love were stronger than life itself, but this was an act of concern and regard that transcended love. Taylor was overwhelmed with a swelling of admiration for Susan that threatened tears from his own eyes.

A terrible surge of panic had gripped Susan when the two wolves disappeared. What she had done was irreversible. Could Gray Girl adapt to a wilderness environment? Had the young wolf been transposed from a world of comfort to one of constant fear and invariable strife. Had she done the right thing?

But the doubts were fleeting. As she thought about the giant protector and his year-long dedication to his young family, the panic passed. The massive black image had directed the moment and he would direct Gray Girl back to her rightful destiny.

"Why don't we eat our sandwiches," she said. Her voice sounded happy, almost sparkling. Other than the quiet tears that slowly trickled down her cheeks, she seemed to have been visibly unmoved by what had taken place before them.

It was as if she had known it was going to happen. That some kind of mental telepathy had existed between wolf and woman and the exchange had been a forgone conclusion. The silent understanding that had passed between them that fateful day on the mountain would not be forgotten —nor forfeited—by either.

"I'm not sure I'm hungry," he murmured. Food was the last thing on his mind at the moment.

"I am," she responded. "This is the happiest day of my life."

"Then why are you crying?" he asked.

"Haven't you ever heard of tears of joy?"

"Susan, I don't know what to say. This is the most extraordinary thing that has ever happened to me, and I've been in the wildlife business all my adult life and much of my youth." Taylor paused, trying to find the words. "I doubted you. I can never forgive myself for that, and I can't expect you to forgive me."

"Don't sweat it, Taylor. It was something that would have taxed anyone's credibility. Forget it." Her tone was conciliatory and understanding. "Tell you the truth, I had my own doubts at times."

"But, Susan, it was more than that. That a gray wolf would confront a human. Not for food or because of desperation or survival, but for one of its own kind."

"It was more than one of its own kind. She was his daughter," she smiled.

Taylor could only shake his head. Being a wildlife specialist who should have had the answers, it was all beyond his comprehension.

Susan saw his bewilderment. "Humans have a word for it, Taylor. It's called love. Animals have the capacity for it too. Perhaps in many cases more so that life's highest order."

They ate in silence, both dwelling on what had just transpired. Susan happy with the outcome of the event and Taylor brooding over his complete misreading of the year-long saga of the Bear Mountain wolf.

As they ate, Susan sensed his self-castigation. "Don't be so hard on yourself, Taylor. What's important is you came through for me yesterday. You were on my side regardless of what the outcome might have been here today. I want you to know I appreciate that."

With a weak smile all he could say was, "Thanks."

There was so much to say, so much to talk about, but the experience of the moment had left them both almost incapable of speech. It was like an anticlimactic collapse of the thought processes. Chewing and swallowing mechanically, neither had tasted much of what they had eaten.

When the sandwiches were gone and the apples eaten, they rose together to begin the downhill hike back to the ranch. Stopping at the same place where they had rested before beginning the mountain climb, they sat and drank. Without verbal acknowledgment, they both felt as if a great weight had been lifted from their shoulders. Susan's tears had ended, and her face was radiant and happy.

"Oh, I almost forgot. Yesterday morning you said there was something you wanted to ask me. What was it?" she asked with a smile.

She was looking at him with those wide, blue eyes, and he was seeing her standing in the doorway of the ranch house looking up at him that first time they had met.

"I wanted to ask you to marry me," he said, without hesitation.

Her eyes became even wider. There was a long pause.

"Are you sure you have come to terms with your personal demons?" she asked.

"I want to resign my position with the Service. I can't advance any further unless I take a desk job in Washington. That's not what I had in mind when I studied wildlife conservation in college. If I stay where I am now, there is no further opportunity for growth. Just the same old same old.

"I've talked to Buck. He said he would teach me the fundamentals of the cattle business. The stock evaluation, feeding and care, ranch upkeep, range work, overhead control. I know a little about personnel management. He's not getting any younger, and he could use some help.

"You could teach me marketing procedures and the bookkeeping. I've already got some new ideas about production that I believe might be helpful and profitable. I'd like to experiment with a couple of other breeds. Some Angus crosses first. See what kind of growth patterns we could establish.

"I've also spoken with your father. Or more correctly, he has spoken to me," he said sheepishly. "He thinks it's about time."

There was a deafening silence.

"Of course, this is all contingent on your answer." His heart was in his throat.

They sat apart at the foot of Bear Mountain looking at each other, the only humans within a ten mile circle. Taylor holding his breath and silently asking God to make her say yes.

Susan's thoughts were not implicit in her eyes, and Taylor had the horrible feeling she was going to reject his proposal. "Maybe we could even get into raising some bison. Wouldn't that make old Billy happy."

"Probably make you happier," she smiled. "Once a wildlife biologist, always a wildlife biologist."

She still wasn't responding to his proposal.

"I know I don't deserve you. I just realized that when you gave Gray Girl back to her father. You put Gray Girl's well-being before your own feelings. Knowing how you loved that wolf, it took incredible strength and resolve few people possess to do that." He wanted to continue talking to prevent her from saying no. "You are the most extraordinary woman I've ever known and the most beautiful."

Her eyes softened as she smiled. "It seems you have spoken to everyone in Montana about this before me. What about Tony and that nosy secretary of yours and Wolfman and. . .?"

"I want to sell the duplex," he broke in. He had rehearsed his proposal speech all the way from Billings the morning before. "The couple who rents the other side wants to buy it. If you wouldn't object I would like to apply the money as collateral for a loan for Tony to open a new Italian restaurant in town. He has his sights on a building and has grand plans. I think he can make a new Tony Gara's the talk of Billings.

"Wolfman White is a dedicated wolf specialist. When he learns of what happened here today, he probably will recommend you for the Wolf Conservationist of the Year.

"As far as Martha McKay is concerned, she has tried to get me married off for the last five years. She would be ecstatic.

"It would make a lot of other people happy too. My parents have worried about me far too long. Pancho and Rozi, Buck and the hands, even old Billy Greateyes. He would have someone to talk to about our wolf brothers."

She was crying again and in his arms shaking uncontrollably. "Yes, Taylor, yes. I'll marry you," she whispered softly. "This is the happiest day of my life."

"You've already said that," he said, holding her fiercely and thinking how close he had come to losing her. Knowing how she had tolerated his indecisions and stupidity, and how much he had to make up for. How it had taken a gray wolf to make him understand what was really important in life. After all his training and experience in wildlife management, the wolf had become the teacher and he the pupil.

The Indian had said it best. "According to Blackfeet tribe, wolves were already in existence when human beings were created. Since only the old are wise, the wolf brothers taught the young mortals how to live with all the beasts. Then the young mortals forgot what they had learned because they were not old enough to be wise."

"You can't learn anything while you are talking," his father had told him years before.

"You'll never learn if you think you already know," Susan had reflected.

The alpha's unyielding yellow eyes had taught him the greatest lesson of all—how little he did know.

The wily wolf had taught him a few other things as well. He had even been responsible for bringing Susan into his life.

What he owed the gray wolf could never be repaid.

"By the way," he whispered into the fragrance of her

silky hair. "After we are married, do you think you could find another name for me besides Taylor?'

"Sure, Taylor," she giggled. "Are you going to kiss me or what?"

****

That night they stood in the back yard looking northward. In the distance, the dark hulk of Bear Mountain was outlined by a Big Sky brilliance bright with dancing stars and a waxing moon. The light rustling of branches with their new leaves forming and the distant gurgle of the creek with its fresh waters from the winter snows were the only sounds.

The warm winds would bring the Montana spring beauty of asters, bitterroot, and daisies, and the greening prairie grass bloom would scent the clean air. Indicators that time and life continues uninterrupted. On this night America's last best place was inarguable.

Taylor was holding her close as if she might escape. Even now, he was not sure she was his at last.

The still night air was suddenly shattered by the full-throated howl of a gray wolf. The chilling resonance came from the north mountain, drifted forcefully across the Big Sky and tapered into slow silence toward the south prairie. Then it was over. Only the muted branches, the murmur of the distant water and a new beating of their hearts could be heard.

Wolves, like humans, have their own distinct voices. Susan recognized the call of an old friend.

"He won't howl again," she whispered. "It was his call of farewell. He isn't alone anymore."

"You think he will ever come back?"

"Yes. It's his mountain. He has nothing to fear now. We'll see to that," Susan said with certainty.

They stood silently for a long minute holding each other tightly.

"Now that he has Gray Girl perhaps we should give him a name also," she breathed against his chest.

"He already has a name," Taylor said quietly.

"Really? How could you know that?"

"The Indian told me."

"Billy? Taylor, how . . . ?"

"He's called Motka."

Because there is a fascination with wolves that is shared by a great number of people and because gray wolves are an endangered species, the author felt the subject would lend itself to the type of story he wanted to write.

Retired after 35 years of service with the U. S. Department of Agriculture, Animal and Plant Health Inspection Service, this is his second novel. He started writing after retirement.

Stanley Moore lives with his wife, Hilah, in Fayetteville, West Virginia. They have two daughters and five grandchildren.

To the reader:

I hope you enjoyed reading "A Wolf Called Motka".

The recent reintroduction of wolves in Yellowstone National Park and central Idaho has triggered a sudden upsurge in wolf awareness in this country. Efforts are now being made to reestablish El Lobo, the Mexican Wolf, in certain southwestern states bordering on Mexico, and the eastern timber wolf in Adirondack Park in New York State. These are subspecies of the gray wolf (Canis lupus).

There are a number of organizations that, having recognized the uniqueness of this animal species, are actively supporting and promoting the gray wolf. Wild Sentry, Hamilton, Montana; the Wolf Education & Research Center, Ketchum, Idaho; Wolf Park, Battle Ground, Indiana; the nationally known environmental group, Defenders of Wildlife, Washington, DC; and many, many other dedicated entities too numerous to mention that are devoted to preserving and sustaining gray wolves in the United States are working diligently on behalf of this animal.

I personally believe it is a noble undertaking and this book's fictional approach to stimulating interest in this endangered species is my small contribution to this just cause.

With unity and resolve in this effort from all of us, perhaps Motka will live on for many more generations.

The author.

A WOLF CALLED MOTKA

by

Stanley A. Moore

To order copies of this book:

Telephone orders: Call toll free: 1-800-375-6161
Have Visa,Mastercard orDiscover ready.

Postal orders: Stanley A. Moore, Rt. 2 Box 6,
Fayetteville, WV 25840-9802
(304) 574-0126

Cost of Book	$11.95
Sales Tax (WV orders only)	$ .72
Shipping	$ 3.00
Total	$15.67

10% discount for multiple orders.
Check or M/O.